The
Enrichment Game

A Story About Making
Data Powerful

Doug Needham

Technics Publications

115 Linda Vista
Sedona, AZ 86336 USA
https://www.TechnicsPub.com

Edited by Emily Daw
Cover design by Lorena Molinari

First Printing 2021
Copyright © 2021 by Doug Needham

ISBN, print ed.   9781634629454
ISBN, Kindle ed. 9781634629461
ISBN, ePub ed.   9781634629478
ISBN, PDF ed.   9781634629485

Library of Congress Control Number: 2021939477

Preface

The Olympic High jump changed forever on October 20th, 1968.

The goal of the sport is to simply jump over a bar raised a certain height above the ground. A young man named Richard Douglas Fosbury had been experimenting with different ways to perform the high jump. When he was in high school, the standard technique of the time was a complex motion of trying to move the body in ways that seem unnatural. He began to listen to the data his own body was giving him. Enriching his knowledge of how the body moves naturally through experimentation, he eventually changed the game forever. His technique of jumping backwards and arching his back to clear the hurdle has allowed athletes to set new and amazing records compared to the previous technique.

Great players in any sport or game see the game differently than mediocre players. This is true in chess as well. Each chess piece moves within the confines of the board. But with a deep and thorough knowledge of the rules and all chess pieces, great players can apply the knowledge of how all these pieces can work together to win the game.

Those of us that are passionate about data management, data governance, and data organization see this as a game: The Enrichment Game. This book intends to teach decision-makers within businesses to see the players, movements, and strategies of the data and software game as individual elements that work together to enrich the whole organization.

Contents

Introduction

From the Uber app that manages your transportation to the social media application that allows you to stay in touch with your distant friends and family, it's clear that software applications run the world. Each of these applications is continuously generating data.

To win the enrichment game, organizations must take that data and do something useful with it. Organizations must understand how all of this complex data can work together to answer questions, do research, provide insight, forecast the future, and recommend new ways of doing business. To do this successfully, data from one application needs to be enriched with data from other applications. Those who can do this successfully can show data in ways that are unexpected and surprising.

The enrichment game has two goals. The first is to demonstrate the value of the data our organizations spend so much money to gather, protect, and in some cases, share. The second is to enrich the data available to a business by showing more context about the meaning of the data. Data strategists, data architects, data scientists, business analysts, and business intelligence designers all play the game. Chief data officers oversee it, and the winner or loser of the game is the business itself.

To understand the enrichment game, we need to know how data specialists differ from software developers in their approach to data.

Software developers create applications to meet the narrow and focused needs of those who need a product developed. A business or enterprise has a portfolio of multiple applications, each meeting the needs of its customers in some unique way. Each application has a constrained set of functions, just like the individual pieces in chess. But unlike in chess, if a new set of functions is needed, a new application can be created, or new components added to the existing application. When a software developer works with data, he or she needs the data to be available to a specific application for a specific purpose.

On the other hand, data specialists want to use all applications' data holistically to further the organization's broader goals. This requires data to be available to anyone who needs it within an organization, not just within the confines of a single application. We must take the data we have and make it better and easier to use. Data Architects will design new platforms where the data can go. Data Engineers will move the data from the applications to the enrichment platform. Knowledge workers like Business Analysts and Data Scientists will create new data products. We want to use data to solve problems not identified in the original specification of the software application. The data of an organization represents both the customer and the future. Using it poorly, not using it at all, or creating data models that prevent future use cases that are known, hampers the progress that can be made with the data.

For this to happen, each application must share some subset of the data it manages. But rarely is application system data stored in a manner that is conducive to reporting and analytics. And when data specialists seek to gather that data to report on any application system, it tends to interfere with the performance of that application.

Thus, the goals of software development and data analytics may seem to be at odds. Therefore, it is always a best practice to separate operational systems from reporting systems. An operational system like an application is perfect for meeting the needs of our customers. A Reporting system takes data from various applications along with some data not created within our applications and enriches the data to create further insights about what needs our customers have.

These two goals of compartmentalization and isolation for the application developer and openness and distribution for the data architect require a balance. Data moving from one application to another requires a governance strategy that allows for accurate data usage in both applications. When the same data is used by more than one application and for reporting, analysis, and enrichment, the complexity increases.

The main strategy for this game, like many others, is that to win you must anticipate future needs. For example, there will be questions that an application's data cannot answer in isolation. The specific demographics of the various users of an application may not be something the application itself captures. Third-party data sources may need to answer the more interesting questions that come up about your users. Additional contextual information about how people use an application is always interesting to other departments like finance and marketing. In addition to building a new application, a separate platform collects the data the application collects. This separate platform is the Enrichment platform.

Data analysts enrich the data available to a business by showing more context about the meaning of the data.

For instance, suppose there is a sudden drop in purchases in one of your stores. What context would help you understand the causes of that drop? Was there a flood? A snowstorm? Road construction that prevents people from driving by your store? Looking at the sales data in isolation can't answer those questions.

Likewise, do you have separate application systems or micro-services that perform a dedicated function for your customers? Looking at data from just a single system can only answer a limited number of questions. Enrich that data with data from other systems, and you have a completely new perspective on both your data and your customer.

The Enrichment Game seems complex, but there are some simple things to keep in mind. Knowing the pieces, the rules, the players, and the board will give you the tools to form a strategy that will win the game for you.

One aspect of this is knowing which data sets are most useful to compare. The book, *Good to Great*, by Jim Collins (Collins 2001) describes how great companies find a single "Economic denominator," such as profit per store, profit per customer visit, or profit per employee. Their example using Fannie Mae found that the economic denominator of profit per risk-level was more useful than profit per mortgage. Their success was related to their ability to understand the risk of default in a package of mortgages better than anyone else. Although this book predates the 2008 housing crisis, the point remains. Comparing profit by these other measures is one of the differentiating factors in defining great companies.

Profit is a measure that has the potential to come from multiple applications. Store information, mortgage information, and employee information for larger companies are all stored in multiple applications. Bringing this data together and making it available to the decision-makers in a simple, easy-to-use dashboard or reporting tool is a significant amount of work.

Or it can be thought of as a game.

As with any game, there are passionate players. I have seen passionate arguments, heated discussions, and downright lies told over various topics I mention here. The game's goal is to make our data as valuable as possible to enhance the lives of our consumers, customers, and the rest of the organization.

Those of us who play this game passionately are a pleasure to work with. This is a simple game where data from one application is enriched by data from another application or even enriched by external sources. The goal is to make the data we interact with more useful than it was before we were involved.

This is the essence of the Enrichment Game.

Enrichment

What is meant by the phrase "enriching data"? According to Lexico, the word enrichment means: "the action of improving or enhancing the quality or value of something" (Oxford n.d.).

According to the book *Infonomics* (Laney 2018), data should be treated as an asset that could be added to a company's balance sheet. Like other assets, data can be enriched to add value to the organization as a whole. This book is about the methods, techniques, and people involved while enriching data for an organization to use.

A software application written to add value to a consumer's life does not and cannot capture all of the data that will prove useful later. An application's performance will suffer if it stores all interaction data from the user for all time, so some weeding out of data must occur. The app does capture most of the necessary data, but questions will arise during the application's lifetime that the application itself cannot answer.

Some questions are simple: Is this a new user? How many interactions has the application had with this user? Is this a frequent user? These types of questions are relatively easy to answer as long as all of the right data is captured, such as timestamps for interactions.

Some questions are more difficult: What browser is the consumer using? What device is the user connecting from? In what ways is this user similar to other users? The answers to these questions must be found by enriching the data.

The process of enriching data makes simple data more thorough. This thorough data, by its nature, is both more interesting and more informative.

The sources of enriching a single application's data are limited only by the imagination. Some examples of other data sources that could be used to enrich data from a single application are:

- Application logs
- Other applications built by the company
- Third-party applications like Salesforce or Customer Relationship Management (CRM) software
- Statistical population data for the user's zip-code
- Social media data that the user may interact with
- Third-party data sources like credit rating agencies
- Other data brokers

Combining this data together makes each interaction the user has with a company part of a universe of data that knowledge workers can explore to look for patterns. This universe of data is called enriched data.

At a base level, knowledge workers can produce reports showing the various important metrics the company uses. Other knowledge workers, like data scientists, use this enriched data to identify new patterns, new use cases, and new opportunities.

Enrichment drives insight.

Insight drives innovation.

Once you change the way humans and machines learn from the data, you change how the data can be used.

We will discuss the various "game pieces," which are sources of data used to enrich application data. Next, we will enumerate the types of other data used to enrich application data and the methods for summarizing data. Next, we will examine the different types of data workers and their roles in the Enrichment Game. We cover the movement and placement of data and the legal implications of moving data around within the enterprise. We will discuss what to do with all of this data once you have it. Finally, we will discuss if you, your organization, and your customers are ready to play the Enrichment Game.

It all starts with knowing the pieces on the board and how they interact.

This book gives an overview of how all the pieces fit together rather than an in-depth look at any piece individually. Every topic mentioned in this book has volumes written about it already. A few Google searches with some of the key terms will give you more than enough detailed information to be reading for quite some time. I will limit the details of many of these topics and only give a brief overview of them. But I will share some of my experiences both where best practices were followed and had a positive outcome and when best practices were ignored, and the outcome was less than positive.

Our goal in discussing these things is to discuss why data, data engineers, data governance policies, data operations personnel, and the tools they need to do their job effectively need to come together in a particular way to meet the needs of the business. It will help you understand why these people, processes, procedures, and tools are needed, in what sequence they are needed, and how to bring all these things together to enrich the data that already exists within the enterprise shows the maturity of an organization. It also shows the maturity of leadership tasked with creating an enriched platform.

When enriching data, it's important not to fall into the trap of spurious correlations, or connections between things that appear to have a strong correlation but really have nothing to do with each other. In other words, correlation does not mean causation. For instance, from 1999 to 2020, the number of people who drowned after falling out of a fishing boat correlates with the marriage rate in Kentucky (Vigen n.d.). But it would be foolish to assume that either of these things caused the other or that the correlation has any meaningful significance. The same can be true of data generated by apps.

Enriching data provides additional value by showing more contextual information around a particular event or transaction. However, the enriched data should be more useful than it was without the enrichment. Does knowing which phase the moon was in while someone bought a flashlight at their local supermarket have any predictive value? It might, if the reason for purchasing the flashlight was related to a power outage that recently occurred, and the person who bought the flashlight worked for a search and rescue operation. A full moon provides much more light available to a search and rescue operation than a new moon. While you may not anticipate search and rescue needs or even power outages if your store is the main supplier for the needs of a community, knowing the phase of the moon may be useful for having some items readily available and easy to find in your store.

One piece of additional contextual information in isolation may not be useful, but enriching data from multiple sources to get a detailed picture that indicates why someone made a purchase or used your software could be quite valuable in anticipating the needs of consumers.

Enriched contextual information about your data provides additional insight into the use of that data by your users.

Many companies have a detailed idea of an ideal customer or customer persona for different situations. These customer personas were identified through survey data and optional questionnaires on the websites. Your company markets to certain personas. What are all the attributes you have identified for your ideal customer persona(s)? Is your ideal customer male or female? Are they a college student, or an empty-nester? Do they live in a city, suburb or rural area? How do they use your products? Do they purchase items regularly, or do they only purchase items to prepare for a trip or an adventure? Does your application capture all of these attributes? How can you enrich the data you have to match data to your customer persona?

The difficulty I have seen with using these personas is that since a persona is an archetype of what a customer would look and act like, no actual purchases could be tied back to a customer persona. For example, at one company I worked, they had an ideal person for whom they created marketing material. She was a 30 something married professional mom of two children. Our application did not collect information on how many children our customers had. Also, we did not collect information on marital status or age. We could derive some of this information based on the purchase patterns, but the data in each application we were using only contained a portion of the persona information.

Relating purchase patterns, delivery addresses, items purchased, survey data, demographic data for the delivery location, and other things got us closer to being able to say, "Persona 1 made these types of purchases," and "Persona 2 made these other types of purchases."

Only by enriching the raw data from each application with data from our other supporting applications could we verify our persona assumptions and even tweak the persona definition based on usage patterns. No data from any individual application gave us enough visibility to the customers' needs to relate purchase patterns to our personas. Only the fully enriched set of data could begin to give us insights into our personas.

The Enrichment platform creates a dedicated place for internal analysis and the opportunity to create new and additional data products derived from an application or group of applications that your business uses to interact with consumers.

CHAPTER 1

Processes

Most people would die sooner than think—in fact, they do so.

Bertrand Russell

Before diving into the nitty-gritty of the pieces and parts of the game, let's take an overall look at the game's processes, so you can decide whether this game is right for your organization.

Knowing where to place each piece and how all of the pieces work together to enrich enterprise data is critical.

Over time, with various implementations of an enrichment platform, the overall process will become second nature. However, this process does need time to mature. I recently attended a webinar where one of the speakers, Peter Aiken, spoke about how he does not like the phrase "Data is the new oil." His preference is to say, "Data is the new *soil*. We can re-use it many times over, but it is not something that returns immediate results. You can't plant on Monday and eat on Tuesday."

Knowing where everything is and what you have available allows you to say, "This is what I have, now we need to be the best with what we have!" Knowing all of the pieces and their current placement will show you where any gaps exist if we need something else.

Filling those gaps is part of the iterative process towards having an enriched enterprise.

Considering potential new use cases gives a solid foundation to know how the data should evolve.

If a man knows not to which port he sails, no wind is favorable.

Seneca

Create a board

There is no board to begin with, only the pieces and a goal. The data model and architectural diagrams, which we discuss later, create the board.

As the game grows, there are many boards involved. Each application has a data model and a data dictionary. Then, the task is to leverage all of the various pieces to get the value out of them. That ultimately creates the foundation that will allow enriched data to grow your organization.

Context is everything when it comes to enriching data. Think of a pawn on a chess board sitting alone. Is it sitting in row 7? Is it your move? Is row 8 unprotected? Suddenly this pawn is valuable because it can move to row 8 and be promoted to another piece. A queen perhaps?

Does your application have the contextual information necessary to understand the value of the data collected? Is this additional contextual information in the Enrichment platform? Data will need to move from an application to an Enrichment Platform for additional value to be realized. Trying to extend an application to provide additional enrichment data will increase the workload and complexity of an application beyond what it was originally designed to do. Keeping an application simple and robust for its users ensures the stability of the application and the loyalty of your customers. The complexity of enriching data and creating new data products is best served in an Enrichment Platform that focuses on understanding the meaningfulness of data.

Draw a map

Have you ever been to a new city and tried to get directions from a local? She says it will take you fifteen minutes, but instead, it takes you half an hour! The local has all the contextual information about getting around town, such as which lane to be in or the shortest distance to locate a subway entrance. To learn to get around efficiently, you first need someone to slow down and walk you through not just what's on the map but all of the other hidden steps.

Likewise, some experts have worked on similar projects to enrich data and create value from it when creating an enrichment platform. There will always be unknowns in creating an enrichment platform. The experts know this and can build a map for getting from where you are to where you need to be. Every expert I know is knowledgeable yet humble enough to know that there are unknowns that need to be faced.

We each have a mental map of how things work and should work. Your map and my map may have different reference points. For example, your friend's mental map of the city includes the subway entrance and yours doesn't yet. Our culture, experience, and expertise define these reference points. As a result, we must work together to draw a map. Having a common set of definitions, terms, and reference points shared among all the players will enrich communication. Teams that work together for a long time tend to share a common vocabulary and share a set of experiences that both enrich and optimize the whole team's communication. For example, if a CDO says we need a clear data model, someone may present a set of JSON definitions when the CDO was thinking of an Entity Relationship Diagram. Ensuring that there are clear milestones, touchpoints, and reference points is the responsibility of leadership.

Having a map to guide your organization in the journey of going from simple reporting to a mature, stable, and reliable enrichment platform will give your leadership confidence that the goal of having and using meaningful data is within their grasp.

CHAPTER 2

Pieces

I once worked for a CIO who said, "Well, data is always the last thing we worry about when building an application."

My first thought to this statement was, "Then why are we building it?" My actual response was: "When it comes to the data platform, we start with data first."

Every business seems to suffer from the problem of competing priorities. When building a new application, why should data come first? The Enrichment Game can identify global priorities so that nothing gets left out. It allows the needs of the overall organization to influence the local priorities of the individual application.

The data our users provide to us through every interaction is how we come to know and understand their needs. The application is just the entry point of their data into our organization. It is the first point of interaction we have with our customers. It is not and should not be the last place that data resides within our organization.

The user provides us with a little bit of data. Taking this little bit of data and enriching it to better understand the user and the world around them is a game with profound winners and losers. It is no trivial game, and it requires everyone involved to be aware that this is the overall game that is being played. Once these various pieces we will be discussing are identified, made available, and made part of the overall data flow within the organization, both the global and local priorities can be aligned and worked on without interfering with each other.

Once again, the Enrichment Game is like a game of chess. Knowing the pieces and understanding where to place them affects the outcome of the game. Some pieces are more valuable than others, especially depending on their location related to other pieces. Knowing what these pieces are, how they move, what they can do, and how to use them efficiently shows the mastery level of the game.

"Take care of your gear, and your gear will take care of you." This is a statement I often heard in the Marines. On a basic level, this means that the more time you spend cleaning, preparing, and optimizing your equipment, the more likely it is that your equipment will not fail when you need it most.

The same applies to data: Take care of your data, and your data will take care of you. How do you take care of data? This starts with simple things such as ensuring you are running the latest software versions, keeping any documentation up to date with the latest changes, and optimizing workflows to ensure that they are stable and efficient.

We will talk about the teams and players a little later, but the team responsible for ensuring that the day-to-day flow of data from one location to another is the Data Engineering team. This team is an operational team dedicated to troubleshooting, improving, and maintaining the production environment with few external project distractions. For purposes of our discussion, I will define the pieces from the perspective of data management. The pieces are:

- Data elements and data catalogs
- Applications
- Databases

A **data element** is any individual unit of data that has a precise definition to be used by the application. In a relational database these tend to be columns on tables. In NoSQL databases these could be elements of a JSON structure. Examples could include, among many others:

- Account Number
- Account Code
- Name
- Address
- Amount sold

It is simply a single property related to other data elements in a table or a document.

A data element resides in some type of **database**. A **database** is a piece of software that stores a structured set of data accessible in various ways. For example, the database can support an application or direct queries to extract data into reporting, analytical, or visualization tools.

An **application** meets a certain need to create, read, update, or delete data to provide value to a consumer of the data. For example, you may have a checking account with a bank. The bank has an application that allows you to see your deposits, withdrawals, and payments. You are both the creator and consumer of this data. The bank may do some additional reporting on a collection of accounts to offer you additional products that you would find useful. Applications have dedicated databases to support the needs of the application. The application itself becomes less of a priority for teams using tools to work with the data directly.

These pieces need to work together in a grand strategy whose goal is to improve the consumer's lives, provide needed information to the customer, and create business value for the company.

These three pieces are not competitive—they are complimentary. *Good to Great* (Vigen n.d.) describes the flywheel concept. A flywheel is an enormous mechanical device designed to store rotational energy efficiently. The flywheel initially resists changes in movement due to inertia. However, once it starts moving, it becomes easier to move it faster. Each item in the following image causes the flywheel to turn faster. You want to improve the lives of the consumer, so you need to understand consumer behavior. As you understand consumer behavior, you can provide needed information to the consumer. This demonstrates value. Identifying new ways to impact the consumer and the customer creates business value for the company.

As you create new business value for the company, you can leverage those insights to adjust to customer needs, improving the consumer's lives. In this case, I am considering the customer and the consumer to be separate classes of people. A customer is someone that is paying our company for products or services. For many platforms that are created, where our customer is essentially "licensing" our products, then, in turn, sell what we are providing along with some of their own unique expertise the consumer of our product may not be our direct customer. However, they do consume the products that we are creating. Ultimately understanding how a consumer uses the product could be a service we provide to our customers.

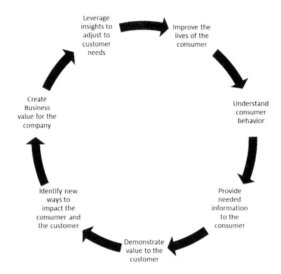

Each turn of the flywheel leads to more momentum. By taking these steps sequentially and ensuring each step along the way is stable, repeatable, and valuable, this momentum carries any organization towards an environment where data is continuously enriched and provides additional value.

The same can be true of the three pieces of the Enrichment Game. Applications, Infrastructure, and the Enrichment Platform itself. New projects or even new components can build on each other in a stair-step manner. Once a foundational component is built and stable, layer more things on top of it. The process of building a step can certainly be Agile, but once a component becomes part of something bigger, it can be thought of as a reliable step that needs to be stable enough for the rest of the stairs to build upon. This approach can change the sequencing approach of projects or tasks, and the prioritizing for enhancements.

One step in the process needs to be aware that there are other steps dependent on it. Otherwise, we build a house of cards that will collapse. Care and due thought must be given to the change and the downstream impact of the change.

A data model for an application is not typically built with enrichment as a goal. The goal of the data model for the application itself is to meet the application's needs and ensure that this application meets the needs defined through requirements. I have worked with many data models. A data model created in isolation without input from a data architect or without considering data governance guidelines tends to need many changes as the data flows into an enrichment platform. Some additional thought about other use cases that are not an immediate requirement would have made these data models much more robust. The simplest example of this is keeping track of when a record is updated. Typically in a relational database, this is done through a timestamp on the record that is separate from the timestamp of when the record is created. By having this built into the application from the beginning, the later use case where a data engineering task is needed to identify what records have been created or updated becomes much more straightforward.

The data collected in the application needs to go to another location to be enriched. One application I supported had many additional enrichment tables for reporting, presentation, and adding additional data to the application. Closely coupling all of the enriched data in the same database as the core application data prevented making reasonable changes to make the application more stable, performant, and reliable.

Before discussing the pieces individually, let's look at how they can all fit together.

Let's walk through a simple example.

A company has one online application that sells dresses to consumers. There is a separate application for this company to buy dresses from manufacturers. Combining and enriching this data brings together both the sales as well as costs. Looking at this data over time hopefully shows a rise in profits as sales rise.

An accurate comparison cannot be made if a knowledge worker only has the sales data but not the cost data. For example, sales may be going up, but profitability and margins might actually be declining if the cost of goods sold rises at the same level. Using this as a starting point, the head of merchandising may see that margins are closing and need to renegotiate with the supplier or look for a new supplier.

Looking at proper trend data and understanding the demographics of the customer may give an indication that there is a product that is in large demand, and you may be able to determine from understanding the types of customers that you have, that customers don't just want a product like yours, they want your brand logo on their product.

This would change the conversation with any suppliers. There may even be enough projected sales to make an outright purchase of a supply company to lock in their availability.

These are all decisions that would not be possible without showing the relationship between data from one application (sales) and the other application (purchasing).

This requires knowing the data elements available in each application, which application manages which data, and what databases each application is using. Bringing this data together into a common Enrichment Platform can provide this new view of the data distinct from what each application can show by itself. As a result, the Enrichment Platform becomes an essential component of the overall data ecosystem that provides value to leadership without the need for any additional work to be done on the individual applications themselves.

Something unknown is doing we don't know what.

Arthur Eddington

Data elements

Data elements are the foundational pieces with which we play the Enrichment Game. In many organizations, the work needed to identify the available data elements, where they reside, and how to access them falls on the shoulders of the knowledge worker. We want the knowledge worker to use her statistics, analysis, and business knowledge to provide additional value. If she spends most of her time looking for data, the additional value she can provide is diminished by the amount of time she spends looking for data to ask and answer pertinent business questions.

This is entirely different from how the other assets of an organization are typically managed. For example, an organization will have an asset tag on the computers they give employees. A record of those asset tags is stored in a cataloging system within the IT department. Wouldn't it be a good idea to have a single location to review all of your data elements as an asset to your organization?

Best practices exist for a reason. Chances are other people are trying to do similar things technically to what your goals are. So seeking out best practices for every step along the way puts you in a position to stand on the shoulders of giants.

Look for best practices in creating all of the elements described below. Learn from experts in the field of data modeling and data architecture. Use the best data visualization tools. Follow guidelines for creating a DataOps team. Organize your pieces in such a manner that when the time comes to make changes, the changes are incremental steps rather than chaotic firefights.

The need for every component of the Enrichment Game is apparent everywhere I have worked. Application development teams may not need these components, but the following are vital to enrich data.

- Data dictionaries
- A data catalog
- Data governance guidelines
- Data engineers
- DataOps
- Knowledge workers

The need does not change; the only thing that changes is the level of adoption and the priority given to creating the various components. Data dictionaries, good data models, well-defined data flow processes monitored by operations teams, off the shelf tools for creating reports—all of these pieces fit well together to solve the infrastructure needs of the knowledge worker.

Understanding what data elements are being collected, stored, and managed in what location is paramount to playing The Game effectively. This is done using two primary tools: a data dictionary and a data model.

As defined in the IBM Dictionary of Computing, a data dictionary is a "centralized repository of information about data such as meaning, relationships to other data, origin, usage, and format." The data dictionary defines how the individual data elements are stored, used, and where to find them. Each application needs to have its own data dictionary. Each data element documented in this data dictionary also appears in a data model. Whether or not an actual data dictionary is created and maintained, the data elements are part of the data model. Collecting these data elements into a proper data dictionary and ultimately a data catalog is an important activity.

The term "data model" has several definitions. Using a modified version of a definition I have used elsewhere, I will define the term here:

A relational data model is a set of tables satisfying at least first normal form, that have foreign key relationships in support of a business subject area for use by an application (Needham, Data Structure Graph: The Application of

Graph Theory to the Design and Implementation of a Relational Data Model n.d.).

First normal form is a technical term that essentially means that all of the columns or attributes of a table are related to the table's primary key. I will go over more details of normalization in the section on relational databases.

A non-relational data model is a set of data elements grouped together in a document, graph, or Resource Definition Framework (RDF) data store to support a business subject area for use by an application. The following figures illustrate the same data structures implemented in various ways. The first one is an Entity Relationship Diagram (ERD), second one a graph database, third one a Resource Definition Framework (RDF) model, and fourth one a Document Database Data Structure.

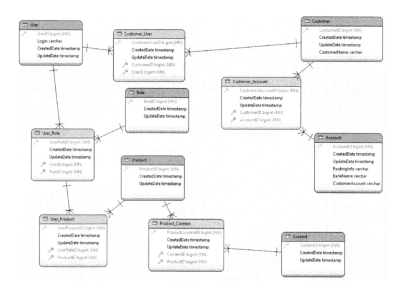

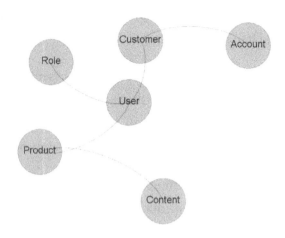

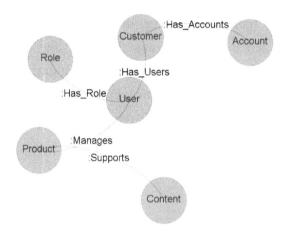

```
{
    "Customer": "1",
    "Customer_Account": ["Account1", "Account2"],
    "Customer_Users": {
        "User": "User1",
        "User_Role": "Admin",
        "User_Product": {
            "Product": ["Product1", "Product2"]
        },
        "Product_Content": ["URL1", "URL2"]
    }
}
```

A relational data model consists of tables that are organized similar to what you would see in an Excel spreadsheet. In this example, each sheet is like a table. The table is in "first normal form" if all the columns in the sheet are related exclusively to the key column that could be used to reference that individual row in the sheet. In the section covering relational databases we will discuss the various normal forms and how they are used in data modeling. A key column uniquely identifies a row in a given table (in this example, a sheet). Another sheet that may need to reference the data in this sheet only has a "foreign key" referencing the key in the sheet.

A non-relational data model does not organize data in rows and columns. These non-relational data models may look like a document, a graph, or another structure that does not conform to this row and column type structure.

All this documentation is considered **metadata**. Metadata is data that provides information about other data. This data dictionary and collection of dictionaries into a catalog describe the data element, which applications are using it, how the applications use it, the access rights to the data, formatting information, and any legal constraints on using, storing, and storing disposing of the data element.

A single document is not enough to describe this data from multiple applications and several external providers. Therefore, it's necessary to use a **data catalog**. A data catalog is a collection of such documents along with information about how to access the various applications.

These data elements that are documented well in things like data dictionaries and data catalogs are one of the primary pieces of the Enrichment game.

Data dictionary

The individual application data dictionary is a document that describes the data stored in the application, how it is related to other data within the application, and what the business meaning of the data element stored in the database column represents. The Description column in the table below is an example of the actual meaning of a column.

For example, in the table below, "Account Key" is a primary key in a table. This key is how this table is related to other tables throughout the application. By only storing the key in other tables, the need for duplication of data is reduced. The user writing a query can simply refer back to the table where this key is defined.

The column named "Account" is the actual account information created by the sales team when they arranged the contract. This could be a system like Salesforce. This data does not originate here, but by ensuring this data flows from Salesforce into this application, the data from this application is enriching the information available to Salesforce. More on this later.

The column "Name" is simply the customer name. Again, this name probably originated in another application. If the customer sees this name, will they want to change it? If they do want it changed in this application, will those updates flow back to the originating system? In the cases of company acquisitions, there may be a need to change the name of a company. I once worked for a startup that 3M ultimately acquired. Our brand was kept on our product, but all business relationships transferred to the name 3M. Making changes to an account and having those changes flow accurately to all application systems within an enterprise reduces workload by making changes to proper Master Data and having that flow to all the applications dependent on this Master Data.

Column name	Data type	Length	Description
Account Key	UUID	16	The primary key of the account table.
Account	Varchar	32	The account number originated in the accounting system for this customer.
Name	Varchar	100	The customer name.

This is a tiny example of what is stored in a data dictionary. Other things may include the application where the data is collected, what happens when this attribute is updated or created, who is allowed to use this data. The basic details of what is stored in the data dictionary are generic for all applications, the enriched details can be customized to the needs of an organization. The important thing is to have one that stores some minimal amount of information about the data collected, and it is shared amongst the application developers, the business, and the knowledge workers who need it.

The data dictionary is very important to the knowledge worker. It allows the knowledge worker to be able to look up the availability of data in one location to answer the questions posed to her. If she has worked at your organization for some time, she may know the location of data without having to look it up, but as the number of knowledge workers grow, will all of them have this built-in knowledge? If some of your knowledge workers leave, will their replacements know where the data is as quickly and easily as your original knowledge workers?

When new people join a team, they must understand the data managed within an application to contribute. Thus, the data dictionary is a force multiplier for any team or individual supporting, maintaining, and enhancing an existing application.

The data dictionary is the starting point for any enrichment services creation. Knowing the available data gives the enrichment team a starting point for meeting the needs of knowledge workers as they seek to create innovations to drive the business forward.

When there is a clear data dictionary that is well maintained, the process for moving data around to get to the answers needed by leadership is straightforward. Identify the data needed for some report or analysis, refer to the data dictionary, run some queries, or create new Extract, Transform, and Load (ETL) processes. The data is available to meet these new needs without putting an undue burden on the application development team.

In organizations where no data dictionary exists, getting data extracted from an application becomes a negotiation. The data owner of the application, if one even exists, must identify all of the columns and tables required. Often, they must take time away from their projects to put queries together to provide to the data engineering team just for a few simple reports. Treating each report as an individual set of queries that has to be created by the development teams that are already under other deadlines unrelated to these reports, makes it difficult to get answers to business questions promptly. In some cases, working on integration projects and starting from scratch to create a data dictionary has thrown project timelines so far past deadlines that the overall business suffered. Features that have been committed to customers were delayed by months.

Having at least a basic data dictionary for each application and keeping all data dictionaries together in a data catalog (which is a collection of data dictionaries for the applications and the enrichment platform), would have avoided such delays. Following these guidelines and maintaining this documentation iteratively would keep things current and useful while keeping the development teams focused on their deliverables.

Application access

When moving around and accessing data and metadata, it's vital to ensure that proper safety and security protocols are maintained. For example, does your application contain healthcare data or other private information about customers? There are some serious regulations for who can see Protected Health Information (PHI), Personally Identifiable Information (PII), or credit information. Consider compliance, security, and privacy from the start.

In some cases, there are regulatory guidelines for application access and storage. Each application will have its own set of rules for who has access to which data and how that data can be manipulated.

From an application perspective, there are security roles to implement. These roles prevent the administration from having to manage the security for every individual user.

Instead, they will only need to manage categories of users. In general, the following access rules should apply:

- Users can interact with their own data.

- Support personnel can access the user data and assist the user in making any changes.

- Administrative personnel can review and potentially modify any of the data within the application.

The enrichment team can view data but not modify it within the application itself. The enrichment team, made up of Data Engineers and Knowledge Workers, will pull data from an application and migrate that data to a secondary system, then further enrich the data. To do so, they will need to access all of the data. Then once the data is in the Enrichment Services Production environment, similar security roles for accessing the enriched data must be established. The knowledge worker will need to have all of the data available to her. However, the data products created should only expose sensitive data based on clear requirements.

Data recording

Each application has rules about what data is stored and what data is not stored. Organizations must be sure that they are recording and storing useful data for future projects.

I have seen many cases where a business question needed to be answered only to find that the data to answer this question was never even captured. In one instance, the essence of the question was how often a particular set of data within the database was updated. There was no mechanism built into the application or data model to capture if a record was updated, what the value was changed from, and what the value was set to after the change. Rather than make an application change to address this issue, my data team set up a process to capture data changes and store them in a separate location that had to be then integrated back with the original reports to show the progression of the changes over time. This was more overhead to the database infrastructure that could have been avoided if the application had maintained the data structures properly with timestamp indicators of when something was updated to begin with.

Clearly understanding the data stored in the application is part of defining the data dictionary for an application. The data dictionary will change over time, but having the baseline document as reference gives roles like the data steward the knowledge necessary to be able to quickly identify if there are questions like the above that can be answered directly from the application data itself, of whether to make a change to provide the appropriate data to the knowledge worker to answer the questions of the moment.

Questions change over time. The questions that the data can answer as applications are originally developed should also be captured as part of the data dictionary. When new questions arise, the first approach should be to try to take the existing data and reorganize it to test if the restructured data can answer the question more efficiently. This approach would save time and effort in the long run if it works and is often the most expedient method of solving the problem.

If there is no way to provide the answers, new initiatives will need to be started to provide these answers. For example, the CEO wanted to know the number of a particular product we were selling across all applications. To provide this simple answer, we created a small project to pull particular data from all applications and then consolidated the data in Salesforce to give insight into product sales. This should have evolved into a larger project to collect more data than just the specific data needed to answer the question. Still, priorities prevented creating this enriched data platform that would have provided much more insight into the use cases that the CEO was interested in. In this case, having a CDO whose focus was on creating and providing an enriched data platform would have been of great value to the executive team.

> *Show me your flowcharts and conceal your tables, and I shall continue to be mystified. Show me your tables, and I won't usually need your flowcharts; they'll be obvious.*
>
> **Fred Brooks**

Data retention

But storing too much data for too long will begin to cause performance problems. Laws like The General Data Protection Regulation (GDPR) and others form the foundation of how data should be retained or purged within an application. Legal counsel should be involved in ensuring that the proper data retention laws are followed within your organization. Create policies and adhere to them for all of the data collected and enriched by your organization. Everyone needs to be aware of these requirements and perform audits periodically to ensure that adherence is current.

Once I was working on defining the data storage requirements for the files that contained our backups for customer-facing databases. We needed to ensure that we had enough storage available to put these files within our data center to respond to customer requests. The vice president I was working with said that we don't need to keep many full backups.

Since these databases were used to generate invoice data for our customers, this data is part of financial reporting and retention data. I stated that we need to keep up to seven years' worth of these backups based on regulations until or unless advised by internal counsel that we did not need this data. The vice president exploded, "What regulations? There are no regulations for storing backups." I replied that federal laws require being able to comply with an audit for up to seven years. Only our legal counsel could clarify if this data were part of that audit to reproduce our financial records.

In addition to the state, provincial, and federal laws, some agreements are made with your customers regarding data retention. If your organization enters into an agreement with a customer to retain data for a certain period of time, some clarification may be needed around this policy. For example, does the data have to be readily available? Can the data be made available upon request? Can the data be made available through other means rather than the primary application that the customer is using? This will give guidance for the backup and restore policies and the long-term infrastructure requirements for the data stores your applications need.

Databases

Data storage, processing, and retrieval are the most important techniques involved in winning the Enrichment

Game. Applications retire, infrastructure is upgraded or retired, yet data is forever. Once data moves into an Enrichment Platform, the data itself and the relationships represented by the data begin to provide its own value.

There are a variety of types of databases available in the market today. There are market leaders like Oracle and SQL Server. Within the past few years, there has been a rise of databases under NoSQL like Neo4J, dGraph, couchbase, and Cassandra. These NoSQL databases are optimized for use cases that do not fit into relational databases' rows and columns approach. However, NoSQL databases do suffer from some of the same limitations that a relational database does. If you have too much data stored in the database that an application uses daily, you will have performance issues. The volume threshold of where performance issues arise is different depending on the type of database you are using, but performance issues will happen.

The best solution to this problem is to have a **data warehouse**. A data warehouse is a well-thought-out database system built on robust hardware or flexible hardware if done in the cloud. The data warehouse keeps all historical data from an application and other data sources, including other applications and third-party data providers.

The data warehouse is typically where I have seen most Enrichment processes store the outcomes of their enrichment.

Whether it is called a data warehouse or not, there needs to be a separate and distinct data repository for running reports, doing analysis, and creating data products away from the application data storage needs. The goals of long-term reporting and high-performance applications tend to be competing. Keeping a data-intensive application performant requires only the data immediately necessary to support the application available. Having long-term trends available for analysis purposes requires all data for all time being available to the knowledge worker. This is separate from any regulatory requirement. The trends that the knowledge worker will be looking at may need all of history. There is some debate on this topic that I have seen. Some trend data older than two years may not be useful for some analysis. In some cases like healthcare, knowing the full history of a patient would be quite different from needing to know the full purchase history of a consumer from a grocery store.

Making data for multiple time periods available to the knowledge worker to create new data products is one of the key tenets of the Enrichment Game.

Data stores

All applications require a data store of some variety. A **data store** is a repository for persistently storing and managing collections of data. This could include:

- All types of databases, including relational, document, graph, or another type of NoSQL databases.

- Simpler store types such as files, emails, and text-based solutions.

These application data stores are the sources that are fed into the Enrichment Platform. The term 'data store' keeps things generic enough when comparing various applications from a terminology perspective. Tools like a data dictionary will identify which type of data store the application uses.

There should be a separation of data storage for short-term operational needs and long-term analysis. Several years ago, one of our customers complained the application we built at one of their refinery plants had slowed down over time and eventually quit working. Our executive team was unable to explain why the functionality had degraded.

During one conversation with the team, the comment was made: "Nothing has changed in this application." Immediately, it came to me that yes, something had changed. The volume of data had changed.

This was prior to the days of the cloud, and this particular application was running on servers on-site. The database server was in a small data center room. I went to investigate. The database had two years' worth of data, and the server had not been upgraded. We upgraded the server, migrated all the data from the old server, and suddenly the application and all their reports started working again.

This was an application that was in dire need of an archive process. The separation of operational data from long-term reporting was the best long-term solution. Keep something like thirty or sixty days' worth of data on the primary server. Migrate any data older than that to a server that was not part of operational processing to be used exclusively for analysis and reporting.

This separation of operational data from long-term reporting has been a problem I have seen in almost every organization I have worked with.

Relational databases

The general-purpose nature of a relational database makes it particularly suited for solving various data processing problems. The lessons learned from tuning a relational database to support applications, business intelligence platforms, or analytics are reasonably transferable between these types of systems. Tuning a relational database to support an application is similar to tuning a relational database to support a business intelligence platform. Once you understand the core principles in accessing and tuning relational databases, this knowledge becomes essential to troubleshooting any problem.

A relational database stores data related to a key together in a table. Multiple tables that store data supporting an application are created and related to each other through foreign keys. Collected into a single schema, this collection of tables is a data model. Data warehouses, financial applications, and customer resource management systems are all examples of applications whose data is stored in relational databases. Most applications have some sort of relational database as part of their back-end data storage needs.

One thing that is necessary when storing data in a relational database is the process called normalization. Normalization is a process of organizing the data stored in tables to reduce the redundancy of data and ensure that the integrity of the data stored within the database meets the requirements to support the application.

Originally defined by E.F. Codd in the paper "A Relational Model of Data for Large Shared Data Banks" (Codd n.d.) There are a number of Normal Forms that are well documented, I will only mention a few here.

- Unnormalized Form (UNF): Data in an unnormalized form does not meet any of the requirements for database normalization.

- First Normal Form (1NF): A table has no repeating groups of data stored within its columns

- Second Normal Form (2NF): A table must be in 1NF, and the data represented in the table must relate only to the key of the table.

- Third Normal Form (3NF): A table must be in 2NF, and all of the data must depend only on the key of the table itself. In other words, if there are columns in the table that relate directly to each other, but not necessarily to the primary key of the table the data that does not directly relate to the primary key should be separated into a new table.

Again, lots of literature has been written about the process of normalization. For more on this topic, I recommend the book: Data Modeling Made Simple by Steve Hoberman. (Hoberman n.d.)

Relational databases have been fine-tuned to work with data that conforms with these structures efficiently. If you have data structures that are not normalized you will have performance problems as the data grows. Database administrators, Data Architects, and Data Engineers are quite familiar with the performance implications of working with non-normalized data, and will improve the performance of any application that relies on a relational database so long as they can design the data structures to fit the needs of both the applications and the database engine storing the data.

Relational databases have several advantages for storing data. Structured query language (SQL) is the lingua franca of data access and querying. Having people familiar with SQL on your team ensures that they can pull data from any relational database. Likewise, many other database types support some variation of SQL to pull data from them into an external application.

Even for applications that do not store data natively in relational databases, the reporting tools that can be used off the shelf need data stored in a row and column type structure to ensure they can query and visualize the data needed for reporting and analysis.

Other data storage systems seem to be popular, but the workhorse of the data management world is the relational database. However, the expertise needed to manage data in a relational database appears to be growing smaller.

Designing the physical layout of a relational database is a needed skill for running applications in organization-owned data centers. Cloud-based databases reduce some of the need for applying best practices for the physical layout of the database. While the actual layout that is being used is virtual, there are still some physical disks that store the data somewhere in the cloud. Cloud-based platforms manage these physical disk performance issues of the past much more efficiently than doing the input/output management yourself. However, cloud-based solutions do not completely remove the need for doing things properly. Keeping data organized in data structures that I will elaborate on shortly remains important for ensuring that knowledge workers easily understand the data. I have seen many cases where databases in the cloud lost the advantages of having cloud-based hardware due to poor database design.

Over the years, relational databases have had additional capabilities added to them to work with documents, text, graphs, and other features. A special-purpose database focused on one storage mechanism or another will perform better in the special purpose case for which it is designed. However, trying to make a special-purpose database solve relational databases' problems quite successfully for decades will rarely be successful.

In every case where I have used specialty databases like documents and graph databases, there has been a need for relational databases to exist alongside them for enriched processing.

Typically this enriched processing has come in the form of some type of data warehouse. A data warehouse generally uses a relational database to store its data. This standardizes the data structures so tools like PowerBI, Tableau, and other Business Intelligence tools can efficiently query.

I will elaborate on some of these use cases in the following sections on Document-based databases and Graph-based databases.

Document databases

For applications that use a document database as their data store, pulling the documents out of the primary database and putting those documents in another database where the data is transformed and aligned to data from other sources is a critical step in gaining new value from the data produced by the application.

In IT terms, a document is an organized structure of key-value pairs that collectively make up something important for an application to use. For example, a Key would be an attribute like "body," and the value would be the text associated with the body of the document. When creating document databases, the structure of the document consists of a known key of some sort, then an unknown value of some sort. The Keys make the document "semi-structured" in that the keys should be consistent across all documents, whereas the values stored referenced by these keys could be a date, a binary flag, some length of text, or just a small string like the word "value."

A **document database** stores documents together in a collection. Each document has a similar structure with certain data elements required and some data elements optional. A document database is an excellent choice when the application is written to display things in a structure similar to what is known as a dictionary in the Python programming language.

These documents stored in a document database make the application quite efficient. Each of these documents part of an enrichment platform will need to be restructured according to the performance needs of the enrichment platform to make the data available for other tools to be able to analyze the documents.

Observing or storing this dictionary item as a document gives the application designer maximum flexibility. So long as a document is accurately indexed, finding and retrieving a document for display and modification is simple. Each document is isolated from the other documents to keep track of all the data necessary for one specific use case.

When working with an individual document, these types of databases perform amazingly well. However, when aggregating by embedded subsections of the documents, these documents need to be copied to other database engines or other processing tools like Spark on file structures to answer the needed questions.

However, document databases have limitations. Pull one or two data elements out of the middle of a document, use those data elements to enrich data from another application, and display the result simply for non-application users to review and you suddenly have a new set of requirements that document databases struggle with at scale. When you are working with just a few documents, this performs nicely. When the number of documents you have scale into the millions, parsing all the documents to gather unique values becomes something you do not want to do every time you need these particular data elements. Creating a batch process to extract this data and store it in a relational database is a more stable solution.

In one scenario where I was working with a document database, each document represented an online class. Embedded within the document were the instructor information and all of the students' information for the various lessons and tests taken.

The question we were attempting to answer was: How do we compare the classes to student performance? Is one class and instructor combination achieving better results than another? The end goal was to analyze from the perspective of student interactions rather than the original goal that the application had to store information about the class itself. This required a massive pivot of the data to answer these questions. We needed to aggregate all of the student information across all classes, identify similar students' behavior, and then report on their performance.

We made a few attempts to do this natively within the document database. However, once we brought the cluster down the second time, impacting every class our platform supported, we knew another approach was needed. Copying all of these documents to the cloud-based database Snowflake allowed us to perform the analysis.

By doing this analysis on a completely different architecture, we were able to isolate our activity to protect the platform, enrich the data with data from other data sources we had available to us, and finally make this enriched set of data available to the knowledge workers we had within our organization. We knew the strengths and weaknesses of the pieces available and how other tools could mitigate the risks. As a result, we were able to enhance the strengths of these pieces and pivot our approach.

Graph databases

Applications that use Graph databases have their data organized in structures that emphasize the relationships between individual data records. The power of a graph database is in its performance for serving an application. Like any application data store, if the graph is overloaded with too much information not pertinent to the application, it will not be as performant as it could be. Pulling data out of the graph, transforming it, and aligning it with other data in an Enrichment Platform will make the data from the graph even more valuable by providing additional perspectives on the data from the application.

A **graph database** stores data in nodes and edges. A **node** is a collection of data elements that uniquely identifies one particular node itself. Through **edges,** or connections, one node can be related to other nodes, and the perspective of how the data interacts with each other becomes obvious through graph visualization techniques.

Since a graph database stores the data as nodes and edges, various properties can be added to a node or an edge. They have a query language that is different from SQL. Neo4J has Cypher, Dgraph has GraphQL+-, DataStax has gremlin. The queries themselves essentially create subgraphs for application usage.

Applications built using a Graph database will use the query language provided by the graph database vendor. When bringing data from an application that uses a graph database into an Enrichment Platform, either significant transformation will need to be done to the data, or the

Enrichment Platform will also need a graph database similar to what the application is using.

Graph analysis, on the other hand, loads data from some source into a graph structure. Tools like Gephi, Python, and R can pull data from traditional sources then apply graph analysis methods like centrality, modularity, connected components, and degree calculations.

Before using a Graph database to solve a particular problem, I recommend using tools like Gephi to experiment with your data to verify that a graph solution will provide value. Identifying a problem that Graph technologies can solve takes some experience and expertise. However, a few questions give a hint about whether a problem is best solved with a graph.

1. **What is the path that a customer takes through our store?**

This is clearly a graph-type problem. If you want to look at an individual customer, you would see one thing. But if you take a large sampling of your customer base and load that into a network visualization tool like Gephi, then you may learn some new things and gain additional insight into the layout of your store.

In human resources, a similar approach can map out career paths and their various iterations.

Learning the optimal path through a set of obstacles would require some iterative path analysis work. A path is about more than just the relationship between two things. It is about the relationship of many things, and how something (like a customer or data) flows through the graph.

2. How does a something move?

Rarely does a package, product, person, or participant move from only one place to another. Each step in the thing moving from one place to another is part of a path mentioned above.

You may think that a product moving from a shelf to a box then on to a truck for delivery to a customer can all be handled by individual applications. This is entirely possible. But enriching this data by structuring it as a graph will provide new insight. In one example of this type of analysis, we identified one location that most of our products physically stopped at during their traversal through our delivery process. This location was where many people repacked the items into their delivery boxes to reduce the number of boxes going out the door. Knowing the flow of the product through this location and anticipating the number of orders helped streamline the human resources scheduling process to ensure there were always enough people on staff to get the boxes repacked.

3. What is the strength of a relationship?

In some work I have done transforming relational data models to graph data models, I noticed the strength of relationships between items. The general trick for transforming a relational database model to a graph database is thinking of each record in a relational table as a node in a graph. The number of edges that connect this individual node to other nodes in the database shows different degrees of strength for a node with a high number of connections versus another node with a lower number of connections.

Looking at these degrees of connectedness for individual nodes shows much more closely related items versus those not closely related.

One of the key differences between a graph database and a relational database is the ability to query on and work with the relationships between items. Each relationship between two nodes can have a distinct definition and even have attributes set on the relationship itself.

For example, suppose Bob and Sue are friends. In that case, you can define the friendship start date on the relationship itself rather than create a new entity that keeps track of relationship dates and the changes associated with the change in relationships. Referring back to our excel example previously, rather than adding a new column in an excel sheet or table, you can give additional information to the edge or relationship itself that can be queried.

A knowledge graph is in many ways an enriched data platform. One of the key differences between a knowledge graph and a data store for an application is that the knowledge graph shows the relationship between contextual information with other contextual information.

A knowledge graph is something similar to a tool like Wikipedia. It can be queried through tools like GraphQL or SPARQL. The data returned from these endpoints is usually in a document format like JSON, not rows and columns type data as is customary in relational databases. Plugging into a knowledge graph and providing some human-readable information for a dashboard or other type of visualization can provide additional contextual information about a property that is unnecessary to keep stored within an enterprise's domain-specific enrichment platform.

Many open knowledge graphs provide data for various domains like sports, movies, and even general knowledge. All this data is available via an API call. The data will need to conform to your specific use case and either stored locally for performance reasons or synchronized in some manner such that it can stay current to ensure your analysis is always accurate.

Building a knowledge graph for your specific domain may or may not be useful. When embarking on any enrichment platform, build a prototype and test its usefulness to ensure the organization's time invested returns some value. Building a sophisticated tool that no one uses rarely benefits the entire organization.

Offense gets the glory; Defense wins the game.

Anonymous

Applications

From the perspective of our Enrichment Platform, any applications developed are simply collecting data to send to our enrichment platform. They will launch, change, adapt, be upgraded, perhaps even be sunsetted and no longer be supported. However, the data that is collected is the most important thing to the enterprise. The data gives insights into our consumers and customers. Software applications themselves are a by-product of collecting data.

Applications exist to solve a customer-focused problem that the business recognizes as adding value to the lives of its customers. Therefore, there is a need for the applications to be stable yet agile to serve the changing needs of customer demand.

The foundation of any application is its data model. Having a thoroughly vetted data model that meets the customers' performance, storage, and access needs is the best step in ensuring that the application serves its purpose. In addition, having a foundation of stability allows for making changes quickly to the user interface, the logical flow of the application, or the business rules enforced by the application.

Once these primary goals are met, the data model for the application then serves a secondary purpose. Rather than simply remaining the storage location for the data displayed by the application, this data model becomes the source for future use cases that may not have been defined during the requirements gathering process to create the application.

Who should create the data model for an application? As with anything, expertise matters. When weighing whether you should have surgery, getting a second opinion by a doctor is important. Getting a second opinion from your cousin, who is a bank teller and watches many YouTube videos isn't equivalent to the doctor's opinion. When I had surgery, each time I met with the surgeon, they carefully explained the problem and how they intended to solve it. Their knowledge of my anatomy was much greater than my own, of course. Still, their explanations were clear, concise, and explanatory of my symptoms and how their procedure would alleviate my pain.

Some people study and work with data models, data structures, and the performance of data systems daily. As with the surgeon, they should have thorough, proven abilities in their field and should be able to explain their processes cogently. Ignoring their advice will do your business harm in the long run.

Creating application software requires data structures to be organized in such a manner to keep the performance of the application optimized. However, these data structures may not be optimal for reporting and analysis. A process called **data munging** can provide a partial solution to this problem. Data munging takes data organized for one solution and reorganizes it to fit into some framework that statistical tools can use to apply their mathematical algorithms to the data. Data munging tends to be done by small groups and can be done on an ad-hoc basis depending on the type of analysis necessary.

A data munging exercise can become the requirement for a new extract, transform and load (ETL) process (discussed in more detail later). Data munging is more reorganizing data locally for one or two use cases, whereas ETL processes are reorganizing data for many use cases. ETL processes tend to be written to be maintained by a group. They are data flows that need to happen regularly and need to run without interruption. If there are any issues with an ETL process, it needs to be resolved as soon as possible to meet the downstream needs of the ETL process.

Business rules

Business rules describe the operations, definitions, and constraints that apply to an organization. These rules determine how data is collected, processed, and stored for any application. When data is migrated to an Enrichment Platform, the data will show how the business rules affected the users' interaction with a platform. The Enrichment Platform can also identify cases when Business Rules have changed. For example, data collected under one business Using the Enrichment Platform to monitor these changes will show the impact these business rules have on your consumers. For example, a business rule might state that no credit check is to be performed on return customers. Other examples of business rules include requiring a rental agent to disallow a rental tenant if their credit rating is too low or requiring company agents to use a list of preferred suppliers and supply schedules.

The business rules of an application dictate how the application processes the data based on user input. These business rules are the workhorse of the application. Data comes in and some processing occurs, triggering other processing. One thing leads to another, and a consumer of an application ultimately gets what they need from the software.

Each of these business rules needs to be clearly implemented, documented, and maintained. Knowing what happens when data arrives and what processes are triggered by the arrival of this data could be important as time goes on.

Understanding what stage in the customer journey the customer is in gives some insight into what data they need, what data should be provided, and what data should be enriched for them. Enriching your internal data to show where the customer is during their journey through their interaction with your application will give your knowledge workers additional insights into data that is generated and consumed. For example, suppose you have several customers that are only at the awareness stage of interacting with your organization. In that case, encourage them to move to the next stage of actually considering a purchase. If you have a customer in the service stage because they have some complaints about a product, you would need to provide them with some incentive to convert that customer to a loyal customer rather than lose them.

While a business rule may be informal or even unwritten, it is valuable to document the rules clearly and make sure they don't conflict with each other. When carefully managed as part of the data catalog, rules can be used to help the organization better achieve goals.

This knowledge of how well the business rules are being followed is critical for auditing and external reporting. If a business rule has been defined and an application does not fully meet this requirement, it needs to be adjusted.

For instance, I once managed the enriched data platform for a telemarketing firm that emailed, called, and sent postal mail to consumers. We collected data from multiple sources, including the federal government.

The Federal Do Not Call list was created during this time. The fines associated with contacting a consumer requested to be placed on the do not call list were staggering, so following this new business rule was essential. Unfortunately, there was no place within our applications to handle such a broad list of phone numbers.

The implementation was simple. We collected all the phone numbers into a single database, then before updating information on our dialing software, compared the phone numbers scheduled to be called that day with those on the do not call list. Any number that matched could not be sent to the dialer.

Every day, management requested a report of how many numbers were removed from the process. This was compared against a different data broker where we purchased consumer information to contact. If the vendor that provided the consumer information only provided us data that was on the do not call list, we could negotiate with them for discounts for future purchases.

All of this processing and reporting was done outside the development life cycle of any actual application. However, this work saved the company hundreds of thousands of dollars in expenditures, not to mention prevented fines that would have been quite punishing.

While these business rules applied to our organization, we created an external process to reduce the number of business rules that needed to be implemented within the application itself.

UX

User experience (UX or UE) is a person's emotions and attitudes about using a particular product, system, or service. It includes a person's perceptions of system aspects such as utility, ease of use, and efficiency. User experience is subjective because it is about individual perception and thought of a product or system. In addition, user experience changes over time due to changing usage circumstances, such as new devices for the user to interact with. In simple terms, user experience is about how a user interacts with and experiences a product.

The user experience can be used as a source to further enrich data for decision-making downstream. This requires collecting data generated from the user interface. Data from the UE might include:

- What buttons are being pressed in which sequence?

- Which screens are never accessed?

- What reports are run and how often are they run?

- How many requests are you receiving for changes within your application? Are they related to data input, data retrieval, or data management?

From this information, the development team might ask themselves questions such as:

- Should we spend more of their time on building something new or integrating an off-the-shelf solution? How will that affect your time to market?

- Is it really necessary to have a custom user interface for reporting?

- Can reporting be managed through some sort of embedded tool following best practices of self-service reporting?

Simply categorizing the types of requests received from users and relating that information to your data dictionary or data catalog will enrich the data dictionary to show which data elements are the most important to the user.

> *However many holy words you read,*
> *However many you speak,*
> *What good will they do you*
> *If you do not act on upon them?*
>
> **Buddha**

Text

Humans today generate mountains upon mountains of text documents. In addition to good old-fashioned books, we also generate text messages, social media posts, emails, blogs, comments on blogs, comments on software applications, contracts, and terms and conditions. All of this written text is a source of data to use in the Enrichment Game.

We need to distinguish between database documents and text data or text documents. A document in a document database is an organized structure of key-value pairs that collectively make up something important for an application to use in the IT sense of the word. On the other hand, a text document contains language in the way that we normally use it. Examples would include file servers, emails, comments within applications, social media, online sources, contracts, agreements, and terms and conditions documents.

You can easily differentiate between a database document and text data if you try to read it aloud. If it makes sense, it's text data. If it sounds like gibberish, it's a database document. That's because a database document is intended to be understood by a software application, whereas text data is intended to be understood by humans.

Language generated by people, for people, is also known as "natural language," to differentiate it from computer-based language (such as Python). A collection of natural language documents is called a corpus of documents. Natural language is generally considered to be "dark data," meaning that it is not stored in a tool that allows it to be easily analyzed and processed.

However, great strides are being made in "teaching" computer software to parse and understand the structure of human languages. This is the domain of Natural Language Processing, to be discussed shortly. Relating a set of documents to something interesting for the business can be done with business keys. This is a crucial step. Having documents associated with customer information, yet not being able to closely relate the document to the customer is a serious design flaw. Something as simple as having a table that relates document location to a customer id is critical for the success of enriching the information available to the knowledge worker.

Applying the various techniques listed below on your "dark data," taking the results of the analysis, storing it in a traditional database platform, and then exposing this enriched data set through business intelligence and reporting tools turns "dark data" into enriched data available for the knowledge worker to gain additional insights.

Text analytics

A few years ago, almost every professional social website showed word clouds. These graphics were composed of the words in a given text or texts. The larger the word, the more often it is used in the text. This is an example of a word cloud generated from my resume.

You can see from my word cloud that I have a significant interest in data and all the things that support a data environment and how to use data for effect.

Word clouds are an example of **text analytics**. Text analytics, applying an analytical process to textual data, is a way to get the important concepts out of a document. For example, it removes stopwords, things like "and," "the," "in," "on," and the like. In the above example, the size of the word indicates how many times that particular word was used within the document.

Doing a word cloud or text analytics on standard off-the-shelf documentation like a terms and conditions document may not provide much value. However, if you have an application that allows you to capture feedback from consumers or even a message board with comment sections, this can be a useful tool.

Pulling all of the comments made by a particular consumer and creating something like this may give unique insights into how consumers value your products. In addition, creating an aggregation like this and showing it to a customer support agent who actively talks to a consumer would give the agent additional insight into the consumer.

For recruiting and job placement, getting an aggregation like this for each applicant would provide additional insight into the experience and expertise of the job seeker. Having this information at their fingertips would enrich the experience of both the recruiter and the job seeker.

Text search

Text search is different from text analytics in that scores of documents are captured and indexed based on their content. Similar to text analytics, stopwords may or may not be indexed depending on the use case.

These indexes are simple yet robust in that they index every word in a document such that when a search is run looking for a particular word, the index shows the text along with the text surrounding it and the name of the document where the word was found.

These indexes can also become quite large. They are amazingly efficient for finding documents that contain certain words. We tend to index data that does not change frequently. Once a natural language document is created and published, it does not change frequently. There may be editions or versions of a document—these can be indexed but they are treated as separate documents within the index.

Taking the recruiting example above, if my resume were to be indexed by a document indexing tool, you could find the words "oracle," "database" and "sql" quite easily depending on the search provided. By proactively creating an enriched image like the word cloud above and displaying this in addition to the search results, this could change the conversation between a recruiter and a job candidate. This enriched information would provide additional insights into the patterns of job the job seeker may be qualified for.

Text search solutions are powerful when the need is to identify documents that contain certain words, but it is not suitable for every type of text document. Trying to use this type of solution for all your reporting and analytics needs puts undue pressure on the text search infrastructure. Further, text indexes are not suitable for frequently changing documents, such as the reporting for a data warehouse.

Natural language processing

Natural Language Processing (NLP) describes the interaction between AI and natural human languages. Natural Language processing uses raw human text as its input: the words you see, read, and write every day. NLP can identify key concepts that the writer of the original corpus of text meant to write. NLP has changed the types of enrichment that can be done on text data sets. By running textual data through an NLP process, you can identify the nouns, verbs, adverbs, adjectives, and other parts of speech used within a corpus of text. There are too many examples of how getting computers to do natural language processing can solve different problems to go into here. Doing a quick search on Amazon of Natural Language Processing books returns seven pages of information. Suppose your applications collect natural language data through comment sections available to your consumers. In that case, your enrichment platform should be collecting this data, and your knowledge workers should be using some of these powerful tools that are available to gain insights into what your consumers are saying.

NLP was once the realm of rooms full of PhDs with a background in linguistics, mathematics, and sophisticated programming techniques. But modern computing techniques now make it possible for almost anyone to learn. NLP can be done on a text corpus using various programming languages like Python, making this technology available in the hands of anyone willing to spend some time learning how to use the processing libraries. The more advanced techniques and tools remain in the hands of researchers as it is for all advanced research topics. However, the fundamentals are available for almost anyone to use.

Summary

These pieces of the game:

- A Data Dictionary
- Application Access
- Data Retention Rules

- Data stores
- Applications
- Textual data

Are all items that need to come together in support of an overall Data Strategy that creates the Enrichment Platform. This Enrichment Platform pulls data together from a variety of sources, consolidates the data in a manner that makes it straightforward to do analysis both on the original data from the source applications, as well as relate that data from the application with other data that may come from sources outside the Enterprise.

Having a fundamental understanding of all of these pieces and how they relate to each other to drive the Data Engineering process is the first crucial step in enriching the data you already have.

The next step requires people dedicated to working with the data separately from the priorities of the applications.

CHAPTER 3

People

Everyone talks about building a relationship with your customer. I think you build one with your employees first.

Angela Ahrendts

In any business enterprise, you hear the statement, "Our people are our best asset." This can and should be true in the Enrichment Game if all participants are trained and working towards complementary goals.

The dynamics of working with the various players involved are an interesting study in and of themselves. The two primary groups of people in the Enrichment Game are "keepers" (mostly defense) and "players" (mostly offense). The first group's primary goal is to protect data from any bad actors. The second group's goal is to manipulate and enrich the data. These goals are part of their reviews, and their personal and professional well-being can be related to these goals and objectives. Some people will have a high degree of data literacy in each group, and some will have less. The various teams involved consist of players and keepers of the data.

Keeping other teams and players involved in the process and gaining their trust and understanding will prove fruitful. By incorporating data that other teams think they own into an enriched platform, these other teams become customers of the enrichment platform.

All teams should be aware of the strategic goals of the Enrichment Game. This will show them that their participation can help them reach those goals and that the enrichment platform can assist them in demonstrating their own accomplishments. In addition, maintaining a strong partnership relationship will give all participants the justification for them to assist in playing the game.

It is impractical to have all of the various players, keepers, data engineers, and knowledge workers report directly to the same chain of command. However, since the enrichment game is something that the entire organization must play, everyone needs to remain involved. Keeping everyone informed of how data is moving through the organization, how it is enriched, and how the knowledge workers are applying the data to solve business problems will engage your workers and participate in accomplishing an enrichment services platform part of a positive experience.

An argument could be made that the Chief Data Officer is responsible for all of this activity, these people, and these processes. That may be impractical for a variety of reasons.

My take is that the Chief Data Officer is responsible for ensuring some rational flow of how data moves throughout the organization. They are also responsible for ensuring that everyone who works with data as either a producer or a consumer is aware of how other teams are using the data and ultimately how the knowledge workers consume the data and create new data products. This can be managed by data governance guidance, continuing education, team knowledge sharing, and other techniques.

Just like the players of any game, those in the enrichment game must engage in training. Giving people dedicated time for training, simulation, experimentation, and learning guarantee your organization keeps any edge it may have in the economy.

In any sport, whenever a player goes to a new team, they have to learn how the new team plays the game. People come to our organizations from a wide variety of places. New players bring new skills and expertise to how to play the game. A veteran player brings a lot to any team, but bringing in new talent always requires both the old and the new players to adjust. Team members are not interchangeable. Take the opportunity to both learn from and teach new players. So long as everyone has mastered the fundamentals of the game, new approaches can be taken to make the team more successful. All of this requires training to implement successfully.

Yes, our people can and should be our best assets. But I am never fully convinced of this statement until I see a training budget.

Fundamentals

We marvel at the skill with which an NBA player dunks, how a football player scores even when opposed by multiple defenders, or how a baseball player steals bases or hits a grand slam. But at its most simple, any game comprises a fairly straightforward set of skills: blocking, tackling, running, passing, assisting, and so on. These skills are taught at the most beginner level of the sport. If all players possess these same skills, what makes one player stand out from another?

The answer is that the pros have drilled these skills over and over again, to the point that the fundamentals are second nature to them. Running, passing, dribbling, leaping over obstacles, challenging themselves with the constant running of drills and training their bodies and their teamwork to accomplish things that those of us who sit behind a desk daily would think of as superhuman. From there, the real geniuses of a sport stand out: those who can see the game as a whole and can take those skills and adapt and improvise on them.

In the enrichment game, all the players should have the same fundamental knowledge of data lifecycle policies, data lineage, data literacy, data governance, and data security classifications. Constant practice and drills are the key to being able to innovate—moving data around, testing backups, and restoring. Ensuring the data is flowing accurately daily, validating that the numbers on a dashboard are valid and meaningful. Getting the results from A/B testing to validate that the models put into production provide value to the organization. All of these are the fundamentals for the data engineers and knowledge workers who play the Enrichment Game. As these processes and expertise mature, new insight will arise organically from the teams that work in detail with the data. These insights will drive innovation, future use, and future value for the organization.

Data lifecycle

Players must understand that data has a lifecycle. It is created at some point in time and copied to various other systems for archive, audit, reporting, or analysis. Some data is "deleted" in that it is no longer active. These deletes are soft-deletes or hard-deletes. A soft-delete is just marking the data as no longer available, whereas a hard delete actually removes the data from the data storage system that an application uses. A data purge is a little more thorough in that the data is purged from the original application where the data was captured and removed from all subsequent systems to which the data is ultimately fed.

Data lineage

Where is data coming from? Where is it going? Is it being used correctly? Data lineage documents the origin of data, the frequency of movement, any transformations or standardization done to the data, and ultimately which visualizations or reports where the data is represented. The knowledge worker needs to know where the data comes from in presenting their analysis. For example, being able to say with certainty that the data in this analysis was collected from applications A, B, and C during the prior four months of this year and consolidated using the following business keys from each application relating the data together.

Data literacy

Data literacy is the ability to read and understand data as it applies to a given problem. Just as literacy of a given language means that you can at least read and understand a textual document, reading and understanding the data used in reporting and analytics is a paramount skill.

I once led a database operations team. Part of our daily responsibilities was to monitor and document the flow of data through all the various pipelines that flowed into our reporting systems. Essentially, we had created our own data lineage product to show that each report was accurate based on the requirements of the report and that each data point flowed through the various transformations to create the reports needed by marketing.

We were conducting an audit of our reports with the lead analyst for the marketing department. We showed the audits we ran each day, the accumulation of the data to create their reports, and how often the reports were run. The lead analyst said: "I see all of what you are doing, and I agree that the audits are accurate, but the data for my reports do not feel right."

The person who said this had built an entire forecasting model running on a Microsoft Access "database" on a computer sitting under his desk. He pulled data from various reports after my processes ran, then did other things that he never revealed to us to munge the data into his forecasting system. The decision-making for the marketing department of a multi-million dollar organization relied on his desktop computer that was not backed up, had no documented data lineage, and was enriched through processes he wrote himself with no additional support or feedback from any of the operations team. No audit done on any of his processes. Naturally, he is now a Chief Financial Officer somewhere.

Not everyone needs to be a statistician when working with data. However, there does need to be a common fundamental understanding of how data is created, manipulated, and reported on. There must be tools or processes that document the data lifecycle and data lineage assists with data literacy. Each player knowing the common business vocabulary from the data dictionary, how and when the data was accessed from the primary application, the use cases of the data manipulated by the application, and how the data flows into other applications or the enrichment platform will give legitimacy to the reports and analysis performed by the knowledge workers.

Keepers

There are several different roles that could be considered keepers of data. I label these roles as keepers because I consider them to be gatekeepers to the data within the application they are affiliated with. The overall goal of the organization may be to pull data from various applications, combine it in an enrichment platform and make that enriched data available to various knowledge workers, but the goals of the keepers of the data are not as all encompassing. Their goal is to focus on their individual applications and ensure that the data within their application meets the application's goals.

Pulling data out of their systems or putting new data into their systems could cause some unintended consequences. The keepers of the applications tend to consider this type of work to be an interference rather than an advantage. The various keepers of the data need to become partners in the process of enriching the corporate data.

Owners

The data owner of an application is the person responsible for ensuring the data is captured, processed, and made available as defined by the product owner of the application.

Data owners are responsible for ensuring that the application they are supporting applies the defined business rules to the data this application manages. The role of the Data Owner may be a member of a development team, but the business owns the data. The title of Data Owner is for someone to be the main person responsible for ensuring the application's data meets the needs of the business and the data adheres to the business rules set forth through any requirements process.

Keeping track of data as an asset is something that falls within the role of the finance organization. The financial valuation of the data requires input and oversight by the finance organization. The Data owners ensure that the data follows the rules set forth. Understanding the value of the data collected, stored, and enriched requires support from the financial organization. There is a whole discipline associated with treating data as a company asset (Laney 2018).

Stewards

The goal of a data steward is to ensure data resources meet business needs. They use an organization's data governance processes to ensure the fitness of data elements - both the content and metadata. Data stewards are specialists whose focus is processes, policies, guidelines, and responsibilities for administering organizations' entire data in compliance with policy or regulatory obligations. Some of a data steward's responsibilities include:

- Knowing what data is available
- Making sure the right people have access to data
- Releasing data to the public as needed
- Ensuring data is used appropriately
- Securing and managing data
- Ensuring appropriate use of a data dictionary

They work together with various administrators, project managers, business analysts, and others to ensure the quality of the data remains high and fit for use, whether in the applications or in the enrichment platform.

Administrators

Administrators keep the data environment stable and running smoothly. An entire team of administrators manages the infrastructure of any organization that relies on information technology. These include network, storage, security, email, application, and database administrators, to name just a few.

All of these various types of administrators typically fall under an operational budget. The goal of the operations team is to support, protect, and enable the information technology needs of the business. The objectives and key results of this team of people emphasize stability and protection as their primary set of goals.

Since the topic we are discussing is enriching data, we will focus on the database administrators.

Database administrators' responsibilities include:

- Supporting new application development

- Ensuring reliability of data infrastructure

- Ensuring that data collected always remains available

- Assist security administrators in enforcing and implementing security rules

- Assisting storage administrators in selecting appropriate database systems

I have worked on projects where many assumptions were made about database capabilities, such as having multiple applications with different usage patterns running on the same physical hardware. Some of these assumptions have been true, while many more need to be adjusted. Having a database server running on a cloud server changes some of the complexity of managing a database. However, it does not eliminate all complexity.

The focus of many database administrators is on the protection of the data. Only the right people should have access to data at the right time and in the right format. These rules, defined by a data steward, are implemented and enforced at the database level by a database administrator. Ensuring this is a reality is not something that can be automated. There has to be a person ultimately responsible for the protection of the data throughout its lifecycle. In many organizations that I have worked with, this responsibility falls to the database administration team.

Players

Each player has an impact on the enrichment process. Therefore, it is helpful to understand how they all work together to create an enrichment platform. There are many players on the field when it comes to enriching data. I only touch on three broad categories below, but there are many others, including project managers, data architects, executives, data engineers, and more. But the three categories of people that will drive the success or failure of an enrichment program are developers, knowledge workers, and users.

Developers

A developer is a person with expertise in turning business needs into stable, reliable, and scalable computer code. Developers get input from project managers, architects, and business analysts.

In many ways, they are pulled in a variety of directions simultaneously, and getting their time to focus on solving a data problem is usually a negotiation effort. However, there are a few things that organizations can do to relieve the pressure on development teams. These include having reasonable documentation like a data dictionary and having the data steward for the applications know the application's business rules. Rather than scheduling time with developers and taking them away from their priorities, the data steward should be able to answer the majority of questions related to how data is managed within an application.

Knowledge workers

A knowledge worker is a person whose expertise is understanding the meaning of the data and how the use of data applies to the organization's overall business strategy. Whether they are business analysts, data scientists, subject matter experts, or researchers, knowledge workers are the primary consumers of the enriched data platform.

Knowledge workers' expertise in the business and the use cases that the data represent enable them to understand best the enriched data they are reviewing. They are the people who are both using the enriched data and creating new sets of enriched data for others to use.

These are the people behind the curtain. Just as in The Wizard of Oz, there is no magic behind a business, just hard-working people using their expertise to understand the data and get information to the people who need to make decisions to run the business.

Data scientists

Data scientists are a special type of knowledge worker. Their expertise is in using sophisticated mathematical and data processing techniques to gain insight from the data.

Not all data scientists have the same qualifications and experiences. While some data scientists can pull data from an API, store it in databases, organize, correlate, analyze, and produce visualizations, not all data scientists have this depth of expertise. Some data scientists and other knowledge workers are limited to working with the available data in the Enrichment platform with tools provided to them that fit with their expertise. Their expertise is valuable enough in its own right. However, the team that supports them is often overlooked when it comes to recognizing the value that is provided to the business.

Sometimes all your data scientist need is more training and experience. I have worked with some data scientists who had limited expertise with Python, big data, or database management. To accomplish their seemingly amazing feats of analysis required many hours of development, infrastructure, and configuration expertise before producing a data product that was useful to the business.

On the other hand, it may be useful to add personnel to supplement a data scientist's skills. Having someone with deep expertise in statistics and applied math can be invaluable to your organization. They may not be developers that work according to the same cadence as an application development team. The cadence of the application development team is usually set according to some schedule. For example, they will commit to delivering two new features or enhancements in the next two weeks. The cadence of a data scientist is different, so long as production data is available, certain analysis can be done within some timeframe. However, this schedule that data engineering and application development work to meet, produce very different artifacts with different value to the business. Each team must be able to set its own delivery schedule.

Users

A user is simply a person who uses the application to accomplish their individual goals. Knowledge workers frequently study application users, beginning with how they interact with the application and the data they add, update, or delete. This data can be enriched in many ways to help the knowledge worker understand the user, how they are using the application, what value the application provides to them, and what future needs a user will have.

In some cases, users are given surveys to understand how they use the application and how they might want to use it. This survey data is an enrichment source, as it must be consolidated together with the actual usage of the applications. Having a number of users say they want to use their data in a particular way, and then comparing that to how they are actually using the data, gives guidance on the gaps and opportunities the application needs to fill or meet.

One type of user that is hard to categorize is the executive. An executive never touches application code, but their vision, strategy, and goals are codified in the various applications to meet the business's goals. They need to understand the data and how the data that is being managed is adding value to the organization. They drive the questions that the knowledge worker is striving to answer.

They are not users in the traditional sense of using the application, but they are consumers of the data the application is capturing that needs enrichment.

Teams

There are various teams involved in supporting an application. Each team works primarily in their own environment, with the output of an application development process migrating something into what is called "The Production Environment." The Development team will create something, test it, get sign-off that meets the requirements, then promote the work from their development environment to production. In production, DevOps will maintain the application and ensure it is available and running according to the needs of the business. DataOps runs processes that copy data from the Production Environment into the Enrichment Platform. Each of these teams is responsible for a different area. Since the goal of the knowledge worker is to provide for reports and analysis of production data, their development work must be done with what other teams call production data.

"Production" is a holy and mythical environment where only the approved are allowed to work. This concept is based on the Segregation of Duties best practice to ensure controls are in place to reduce the risk of fraud and error.

There is not a single production environment. There are multiple depending on the use case. Each application has its own set of privileges, rights, and restrictions. Likewise, they each have their own set of administration or operational teams.

It's important to distinguish between production data and development data.

Development data, or test data, is used while the application is being created. During application development, "test" data is populated within the application to verify its functionality. This test data aims to verify all the business rules, data storage, and application functionality rules. It can also assist in the design of data dictionaries.

On the other hand, production data is generated by actual end-users of the application once the application has been released.

It is important to keep these two types of data separate. Test data should not flow permanently into an enrichment platform. The purpose of test data for the application is to verify functionality. The purpose of data in the enrichment platform is to draw new insights from how customers use data. Unless there is a very sophisticated test methodology that simulates typical customer use, the test data in the application will be useless for any type of data product that would need to be developed.

Once sophisticated data science models start being created, they require this production data. If a statistical model is applied to development data, the only thing the statistical model will produce is the type of patterns that the development data ultimately represent. If you are looking for usage patterns for your users and all you have is development data, you will see usage patterns that reflect when the developers worked on the application. These will not be real user patterns.

I mentioned earlier the idea of a stair-step development process. The first step is getting an application in production. Once that step is built, that application will continue to grow and adapt according to the needs of the business. That step is then treated as input to follow-up steps where the data is enriched, reorganized, conformed, analyzed, and reported on.

Approaching development efforts in this manner creates a stable iterative implementation environment where new data products can be created rapidly independently of the needs of any application development lifecycle.

One other way of looking at this stair-step process is developing an application and developing an enrichment platform as separate projects. The enrichment platform is dependent on the application development process being complete for some version of done.

This enrichment services production environment is used by business analysts and data scientists and managed by data engineers. Like any game, the more you play, the better you get. The more often your teams restore database backups, transfer data from one production system to another, simulate failures, and work on recovery, the better the team will play the game.

Each specialty team involved has a different area of responsibility and different goals and objectives. Therefore, forcing one specialty team to follow the goals and objectives of a different specialty team will not produce positive outcomes.

Development

Developers' goal is to create applications. A development team usually consists of more than just developers—there are project managers prioritizing work, business analysts clarifying requirements, and infrastructure expertise ensuring the environment is running accurately. Indeed, in today's application landscape having only one or two developers to write code for user experience, business rule implementations, back end processing, and data flows throughout the enterprise is hardly an efficient approach. Instead, many development teams will be associated with an application.

Developers spend much of their time gaining expertise in one or two programming languages like Go, Scala, Java, or Python. There is a need for application developers to understand the various browsers and mobile user experience standards that are technical requirements for keeping applications robust and stable in the ever-evolving application environment. Each of those teams needs to have a bit of structure to work with.

The data models and data dictionaries mentioned above allow the application developers to work seamlessly with the data engineering and data enrichment teams.

DevOps

DevOps (a clipped compound of "development" and "operations") is a software engineering practice that aims at unifying software development and software operation. Once an application is developed, it must be deployed and made available to the users. The main characteristic of the DevOps movement is to strongly advocate automation and monitoring at all steps of software construction, from integration, testing, releasing, deploying, and infrastructure management. All of this work improves the stability of the production application environment, ensuring it is available for the consumers to use. DevOps aims at shorter development cycles, increased deployment frequency, and more dependable releases in close alignment with business objectives.

DataOps

DataOps is a recent name given to a group of people that monitor data flow through an organization. This is the type of team I have worked on for many years. They usually get alerts in the middle of the night that a process moving data from one application to another has an issue, and they have to log in and fix it. Over the years, DataOps works to automate as many processes as possible. The DataOps team works to improve the quality and reduce the cycle time of data analytics. DataOps applies to the entire data lifecycle from data preparation to reporting and recognizes the interconnected nature of the data analytics team and information technology operations. When there is a need to add a new data feed to the Enrichment Platform, data engineers work together with other teams to create automated processes to move data from one place to another. If data is already available in the Enrichment Platform, the knowledge worker can begin their analysis of the data. If not, the data needs to be brought in by data engineers that work on the DataOps team to ensure the data is available. DataOps utilizes statistical process control (SPC) to monitor and control the data analytics pipeline. With SPC in place, the data flowing through an operational system should be constantly monitored, audited, and verified to be working.

DataOps is not tied to a particular technology, architecture, tool, language, or framework. It is, however, their job to protect the data infrastructure, the data flows, and the data representations that the knowledge workers, the applications, and ultimately the company and customers rely upon. In addition, having a team dedicated to monitoring, enhancing, fixing, and replaying data flows increases the organization's stability.

These teams tend to manage what are called ETL (Extract Transform and Load) tools. These tools are the pipelines that manage how data flows through an organization. If these tools do not exist, Data Ops teams create them. This requires standardizing an enterprise on a toolset, then periodically reviewing that standard to ensure it meets the current state of the art increases efficiency for moving data throughout the organization.

The Data Ops team are the people that are called if there is any problem with any data flows throughout the organization. Their skills are focused on the tools associated with data movement and process control to support knowledge workers using the tool ecosystem to create data products for knowledge consumers throughout the organization.

One of the many process control techniques to apply to data operations procedures is six sigma. As mentioned before, this manuscript is just a survey of various topics and how they all fit together to build an Enrichment platform. Six Sigma is a huge topic with volumes written on it, so I will only give a teaspoon sip of what Six Sigma is all about here.

Following some of the principles of Six Sigma, any system that will be running constantly is defined accurately, key aspects of the processes are measured and the data collected, the collected data is analyzed constantly in case of any defect, improvement, or optimization of the process is identified by the process engineering team, and statistical process control is implemented to ensure that the quality level is maintained.

Too many organizations I have worked in have overlooked improvement and optimization. When an opportunity for optimization is identified, it should be treated as something just as important as any business requirement provided by a business analyst.

In intense conversations, I have debated implementing an optimization technique, only to be told that customer requirements drove the only changes that would ever be made. A customer is rarely going to say: "Just make things better for me." Suppose an optimization technique can be identified related to the structure of the data store or some form of maintenance that may cause a minor disruption but ultimately be better for every application user. In that case, this should be treated on par with a customer requirement. Otherwise, catastrophic failures can occur that could have been prevented with some regularly scheduled maintenance.

Summary

These are some of the people that protect and organize the data of the organization. These players and teams work behind the curtain to ensure that the data flows to where it needs to flow. In many companies that I have worked with and supported, these people tend to be hidden in plain sight and seldom get the credit they deserve for ensuring that the data of the organization maintains its usefulness to each of the various applications that have certain data needs that are met by the movement of data maintained by these teams.

These teams ensure that data that is not supposed to move does not move anywhere, likewise for data that needs to move from one location to another, they ensure that data moves to the right place at the right time and in the right format.

CHAPTER 4

Movement

How do you get to Carnegie Hall? Practice.

The goal of every movement is to move from one stable position to another stable position.

In Martial arts, if you are unstable, your enemy can throw you to the ground. Every movement appears to focus on agility, but the true focus is on stability. Stability allows for agility. Jumping around to show how agile you are will get you knocked down if you have no stability.

A boxing match appears to show two fighters dancing around and showing off their ability to move quickly and decisively. However, if you look at the placement of their feet and legs, you will see another story. Each step keeps the fighter stable. With each step, their legs, thighs, and hips support their shoulders. When a fighter throws a punch, the power of the punch comes from the feet. While the fist is moving towards the opponent, the feet are pressing down, ensuring that the fighter has a stable foundation such that the force striking the opponent does not knock the striker backward.

Stability allows agility. Adaptability requires a firm stable foundation.

Being able to anticipate the future needs of the business accurately can only be done from a position of stability. Knowing what data is available, where the data is coming from, where it is going, and how the data was collected according to business rules gives an organization the stability they need to anticipate future gaps for what consumers may need based on their analyzed behavior over time. Every layer of the architecture has a different degree of flexibility. Moving from one application to another must serve a purpose—otherwise, why is it moving? This section will cover the primary reasons and methods for moving around data in a stable manner.

There are three basic movements needed in the Enrichment Game. In the opening moves, your organization must figure out how to move application data into a separate area where it can be analyzed. In the midgame, you need to combine data from multiple sources to give the data context. The endgame is the moneymaker: analyzing the data to gain insights into how your company functions and how it can improve.

Opening

The opening of the enrichment game begins with a single application designed to meet your customers' needs. Once that is in place, there are a number of ways in which moving the data can add value to your company.

Simple reporting

When an application is first created to meet the needs of a data consumer, the simplest type of reporting consists of a few basic reports from the data store used by the application itself. For example, *how many of product x was purchased* yesterday? This is a very simple question that would not tax the database underlying the application.

From there, the simplest form of enrichment is creating a separate database for reporting and analysis. This database keeps a copy of data across all time periods distinct from the database that the application uses during normal operations. Creating a separate bit of infrastructure for reporting and analysis requires time, people, and money. Early on, while growing a company, this infrastructure is always lower in priority than getting new customers, growing the business, and adding features based on customer requests. But at some point in every application, I have supported, there comes a time when migrating to a new architecture is cheaper, more efficient, and less risky than maintaining the approach of writing application code to create reports from within an application.

Adding tools

I have seen cases where tool vendors claim to reduce time to market for application reporting. In many cases, there is value to adopting a tool-based approach. For example, plugging a PowerBI or Tableau dashboard directly into an application can be a value-add. However, this ties the performance of these reports to the performance of the application. If you have a sophisticated dashboard pulling data from across the application, it will cause other performance issues that will need to be addressed.

You can reduce some of these performance risks by doing database copies or table-level extracts of data for the tools to use. This is touched on in the later section when talking about operational data stores.

Third-party

When the business's need for understanding data grows beyond the application's capabilities, some will package up all of the application data and ship it off to a third-party analytics company.

The advantage of this strategy is that your own employees do not do some portion of the work. This saves your company the need to hire or train your own data experts.

On the other hand, managing a project of this size is almost as complex as creating a data warehouse from scratch within your organization. All of the business rules discussed previously have to be discovered and documented. Data extracts need to be created and delivered. Then the third party has to have time to create their reports and analysis. Remember the previous Soil comment? "You can't plant on Monday and eat on Tuesday." It takes some time to create a process that moves data from one location to another. Once the data is moved from one place to another, it must be audited to accurately reflect where it came from. Then new reports or analysis needs to be done. Time must be set aside for the creation of new processes.

Further, the entire analysis process becomes a black box. If there is a need to migrate away from this third-party analytics company, any new analytics vendor will have to duplicate much of the work already done.

A key element of using a third party is to ensure some dedication is given to skills transference. Your team may never achieve the same level of expertise as the analytics provider. Nevertheless, having them walk through their process at a peer level to show how they create value will give your team greater expertise as you grow your analytics capabilities. Have their knowledge workers spend time with your knowledge workers. Their data engineers should work with your data engineers and their visualization experts should work with your visualization experts.

The more people that understand the processes, techniques and tools that are used, the better. All organizations have turnover, but duplicated knowledge ensures that the overall domain knowledge will be balanced over time regardless of whether the turnover happens in the analytic provider or within your organization.

Carefully consider the advantages and disadvantages of outsourcing your data to a third party. Is it worth it to grow your own in-house expertise? Or is it simpler to provide additional data to a third party that may or may not have your companies best interest at heart? In one case, while working with third-party analysis vendors, when they got a new and much larger client, their responsiveness to our requests for changes was responded to with less efficiency than when we were a new customer.

Midgame

Our goal of the midgame is to start to do new things with the data, separate from what is done with the data in the application. When entering into the Midgame, one of the decision points is to decide which type of approach will enrich the data effectively and make it useful beyond the applications. Some standard approaches generally fall in the data warehouse category that I will describe with some technical detail. While this is just a survey of these approaches, it is important to understand some of each approach's detailed differences and strengths. Each step deeper into the game increases both the complexity and the ultimate value that can be gained from the data.

Once the production data from the source application(s) enters a development data engineering area, the opening is complete. This is where we start to do new things with the data separate from any application requirements.

This can involve taking data from a single application, reorganizing it, and combining it with data from external sources. That external source can be another application within the enterprise, data from the semantic web (machine-readable data available via the internet), or data provided by external vendors paid for by the Enterprise.

This integration layer is one of the most interesting data engineering challenges of any Enterprise.

Data lineage

Knowing where the data is coming from (data dictionary), what transformations are happening (source to target mappings described below), and how frequently data is being copied (data flow specifications) are part of this process. These details make up **data lineage**.

To move data from one application to another application or enrichment platform, it must be made clear where the data is coming from, where it is going, and any changes that need to be made to the data to make it useful to the target system. One of the most straightforward mechanisms that capture this information is called a source-to-target map.

Source System	Source Table	Source Column	Source Data type	Transformation Rule	Target Table	Target Column	Target Data type

The Source System is the application or database schema from which a single data element is captured.

The Source Table and Source Column are the table and column where this data is stored. For structures like JSON entities or Graph databases, this could be the entity names or nodes and attributes, respectively.

The Source Data Type may or may not be needed, but when creating relational tables, it is important to ensure that either the data types for both source and target columns match or the target is larger than the source. Otherwise, the data could be truncated, and the process would have to be redone from the beginning.

The Transformation Rule describes how the data from one source column would need to be changed for the target column. This could be system-generated in the case of timestamps, or some logic that would transform a single column into multiple target columns.

The Target Table and Column are where the data is stored.

This is a simple example and could be expanded depending on the number of systems, the transformation rules needed, or other reasons. What remains important is having some form of lineage document that can confirm that the data flows from System A flows into System B accurately. An operations or data quality process would need this type of information to validate and verify that data is moving in the expected manner.

This integration layer could be named many things. Some examples follow, but the objective for all of these is to be a data-focused, centralized, consolidated database used specifically to produce downstream data products.

Data vault

Data vault modeling is a database modeling method designed to provide long-term historical storage of data coming in from multiple operational systems. It has built-in capabilities for auditing, data lineage, loading speed, and resilience to change. Data lineage is a critical aspect of a data vault. This means that every row in a data vault must be accompanied by record source and load date attributes, enabling an auditor to trace values back to the source. It was developed by Dan Linstedt.

Data vault modeling makes no distinction between good and bad data ("bad" meaning not conforming to business rules).

A data vault is designed to enable parallel loading as much as possible so that immense implementations can scale out without the need for major redesign.

Creating a data vault is the best solution when you need a robust, repeatable, auditable, integrated data layer that can adapt to changes quickly.

A dimensional model has only two types of tables Facts and Dimensions. A data vault has only three types of tables: Hub, Link, and Satellite.

A Hub table captures the business keys of an application.

A Satellite table captures the contextual information of either a business key or a relationship among business keys.

A Link table captures the intersection of two or more business keys.

By keeping these items separate, the Data Vault approach is very robust in a changing environment. For example, suppose new contextual information is provided in an application. In that case, that data can be dealt with by creating a new Satellite table and relating it to the business keys through either a direct relationship or through a Link table.

There are automation tools for creating the processes based on metadata and source to target table mappings for creating and maintaining a stable data vault implementation.

Monitoring the data vault load processes by the DataOps team is paramount to success.

A Data Vault is not typically exposed directly to reporting tools unless you have some sophisticated tools that can work with database structures other than dimensional tables. The value of the Data Vault is in high-speed ingestion, parallel loading, consolidation of data from multiple systems simultaneously, and full auditability. Systems specifically for OLAP analysis and reporting are generally populated from a data vault after accurately capturing all of the raw data from the source applications.

Dimensional model

The most efficient data model for doing reporting from a relational database is a type of data model called the **dimensional data model**. A dimensional model breaks reporting data structures down into two major types: a dimension table and a fact table.

A dimension table contains the textual descriptions of the business. Dimension tables are tables that do not conform to the normalization process we covered in the section on relational database. These tables have many columns and few rows with as much descriptive information as possible to describe a concept or create enhanced contextual information describing things that are being measured.

Let me provide an example of a dimension using date information.

DateKey	Year	Quarter	Month	Day	WeekOfYear	DayOfWeek
20210101	2021	Q1	January	01	Week1	Friday
20210102	2021	Q1	January	02	Week1	Saturday
20210103	2021	Q1	January	03	Week2	Sunday
20210104	2021	Q1	January	04	Week2	Monday
20210105	2021	Q1	January	05	Week2	Tuesday
20210106	2021	Q1	January	06	Week2	Wednesday
20210107	2021	Q1	January	07	Week2	Thursday

Every programming language has date functionality, including SQL. Why is it important to create a date dimension for reporting and analysis? How does this enrich the data?

When a small number of records are analyzed, doing a date calculation to convert a date stored as a timestamp into the day of the week, or week of the year, month, or even quarter probably has a small performance overhead.

When there are billions of rows of data, this calculation is done a billion times every time a query is run. When specifically looking for information programmatically (like "Show the number of transactions that happen every Tuesday"), these timestamps would have to be converted, then filtered, and then some indicator of the week of the year would have to be calculated. By precalculating different ways of describing the date and time, the queries can be run using this enriched table and filtering on the data specifically using an optimized index.

In this example, we are talking about something simple like days, weeks, and months, but this structure is the same if we were grouping products into various categories or other types of dimensions. By creating separate contextual (dimensional) tables that describe your data in different ways, you can look at the same data from different perspectives or even multiple perspectives at the same time if different dimensional data is provided from different application systems.

Doing various group by functions in SQL will return the data ready to be loaded into time series analysis tools. Most business intelligence tools that describe themselves as OLAP (On-Line Analytical Processing) tools generally require data to be organized into a star schema or dimensional data model.

This assumption about the data structures allows these tools to generate amazingly efficient queries based on this type of semantic definition of the type of data to which they will be connected.

Dimensional tables also have one additional feature. There are some default values populated in the table as part of defining the table. This is done before loading data from the source. At a minimum, having a default key of the number 1 and the text description populated with the text value "NULL" allows a dimensional data model to always use inner joins when relating data between facts and dimensions. The inner join is more efficient for various reasons and takes less processing time to tie the data together. When a fact table is joined to some dimension that may not be populated in the original data, rather than having the value be a NULL, it is actually the text "NULL" to identify where data may be missing.

A fact table is where numerical performance measurements of the business are stored. Fact tables are narrow, long tables that contain a row for each measure based on every dimension necessary to report, analyze or display the data represented in the fact table.

There are a few other cases for the default values that should be taken into account depending on your use cases, but the Kimball Group's design tips (https://www.kimballgroup.com/2010/10/design-tip-128-selecting-default-values-for-nulls/ n.d.) provide clear evidence that these values are needed.

Ralph Kimball and Margy Ross's book *The Data Warehouse Toolkit* is an excellent resource for learning and applying all the details associated with dimensional modeling.

Here is a tiny example fact table.

Customer Key	PurchaseDateKey	ItemKey	Quantity	Cost	Tax
451	20210101	5	3	5.15	.23
42	20210102	7	6	11.89	.67
108	20210103	11	9	25.67	1.49

The keys are related to the dimensions described earlier. Creating a stable set of dimensions that are conformed to work together to produce a common set of contextual information for your reporting needs is an entire discipline within data architecture.

The query to gather data together and group by any field in the dimension table is a single join along with a group by clause in your SQL statement.

While this example is trivial, with just a few attributes shown as the dimension tables grow in width, each column enriches the context of the depth of the data in the fact table.

In one organization where I was doing a demo of how to improve their reporting performance, I created a single fact table with nine dimensions and two fact tables. Then, I demonstrated how to replace dozens of stored procedures with a few queries against these well-organized tables with consistent performance regardless of the type of report the user had requested.

The Date dimension alone was the table that was queried the most often in these queries. This showed that the customer was most interested in seeing data over time. By eliminating the calculations needed to convert dates by using a robust date dimension, the types of data we were demonstrating in the dimensional data model far exceeded the performance capabilities of the stored procedure approach.

The goal is not to eliminate the need for application developers to write reports. Instead, the goal is to enrich both the data and approach for solving problems to make things more efficient.

There are various nuances of both dimensions and fact tables, but structurally they remain the same. Thus, any type of reporting and analysis that a relational database can support can be done efficiently by a dimensional data model, so long as the data is transformed and loaded into these structures on an ongoing basis.

A dimensional model can directly support an application or be populated by some of the other data structures mentioned below.

Because there are only two types of tables, the read queries for a dimensional model are quite efficient. The various database query optimizers have only simple joins and index lookups to perform to produce a report.

Imagine a world where creating a new report or piece of analysis is straightforward and efficient. Answering questions becomes the speed of using a nice reporting interface, dragging data elements onto a screen, organizing those data elements by time, then plotting trend lines to see the behavior of a data point.

The complexity of doing the reporting or analysis work is not changed. However, it is made part of a standard process. Transforming data into new structures makes the work of the knowledge worker efficient and seamless without the need for constant adjustments by the application development team to their development timelines.

We will revisit this topic when we discuss self-service reporting.

Operational data store

Creating an operational data store for your application's data improves the application's performance by moving day-to-day reporting functions to a separate database maintained by the data ops team. The amount of data that needs to be summarized for daily reports will only continue to grow, and performing these reports on databases that will not interfere with your application systems will reduce the risk of interfering with your customers and give you the most important up to date information in a reliable, stable, and repeatable manner.

An Operational Data Store (or "ODS") is used for operational reporting that focuses on the companies' day-to-day functions. An ODS is a database designed to integrate data from multiple sources for additional operations on the data, for reporting, controls, and operational decision support. Unlike a production master data store, the data is not passed back to operational systems. It may be passed for further operations to the data warehouse for reporting.

An operational data store will take transactional data from one or more production systems and loosely integrate it. It is still subject-oriented, integrated, and time-variant. Still, the data structures will not change as drastically as if the data were migrated to something like a data vault or dimensional model.

Because the data originates from multiple sources, the integration often involves cleaning, resolving redundancy, and checking against business rules for integrity.

An ODS is usually designed to contain low-level or atomic (indivisible) data (such as transactions and prices) with limited history that is captured "real-time" or "near real-time" as opposed to the much greater volumes of data stored in a data warehouse generally on a less-frequent basis.

Most operational data stores I have worked with are little more than copies of application databases stored in a single database with no time limitations. W. H. Inmon's *Building the Operational Data Store* describes the star schema as the most efficient operational reporting. Having an operational data store where both raw data from the operational systems is stored and having this ODS transform the data into a dimensional model for reporting and decision support is considered a best practice for clean, stable, and consistent reporting (Inmon 1999).

Data lake

A **data lake** is a system or repository of data stored in its natural or raw format, usually binary large objects (blobs) or files. A data lake is usually a single store of data including raw copies of source system data, sensor data, social data and other types of data that does not fit into relational data structures. A data lake can include structured data from relational databases, semi-structured data, unstructured data, and binary data. This transformed data is used for reporting, visualization, advanced analytics, and machine learning tasks. This is where the data begins to produce additional value.

Structured data is organized data that easily fits into the rows and columns of something like an Excel spreadsheet. Unstructured data is just a file, an image or a photograph, voice recording, video footage, or sensor information. Semi-structured data has some elements of a structure embedded in the file itself and consists of structures such as email contents, social media posts, and even some documents stored in pdf or docx structure. It is semi-structured because it has an organization to the data; however, the data itself does not easily fit into the rows and columns approach that most people think of when looking at data.

All of these pieces of data can be related to each other, but there is some transformation or munging effort that needs to take place to relate the unstructured and semi-structured data to the structured data. Even some structured data requires labor. If it lacks contextual information like data dictionaries, data lineage documentation, and other defining information, even structured data may challenge our understanding.

Because of the volume, velocity, and variety of data that could be stored in a data lake, newer technologies such as Hadoop have been needed to keep costs down and access stable. Choosing to adopt a newer technology requires a well-thought-out approach within the enterprise's data ecosystem. Adopting new technologies without training is a gross oversight. During the decision process for choosing a new technology, time and training are primary factors for deciding.

Creating a data lake is a straightforward process— determining if you need a data lake and what specific problems it will solve will require due thought of the business. However, one thing that cannot be emphasized enough is to ensure that if the decision is made to go forward with a data lake, it must have a clear objective, and the teams that will be working on it will require training to ensure it is a success.

We are in the endgame now.

Doctor Strange

Endgame

Lastly, all of this well-stored, well-organized data must be enriched so that it adds value and helps the organization solve problems. For now, the state-of-the-art method for Data Enrichment is analytics. Analytics is where we take all this enriched data and apply statistical methods to identify groups of users, usage patterns, and similar products that are purchased together. Analytics is where we start to do the things that gain the insight that drives your business forward.

There are ways of enriching data without using external data sources. Simply changing the way the data is aggregated could give new insights into user behavior. For example, in looking at the sales averages by location, you can quickly see interesting things like how one store is doing quite well, while another may need some attention. Grouping and segmenting customers and comparing individual customers to the group or segment will show behavior trends and patterns.

Another way of enriching data is running tests on the application itself to determine how to change the applications. Applications can be enriched through simple testing. Everything presented to the application user could be tweaked and analyzed through simple tools like A/B testing. With A/B testing, certain features within an application can be tested to determine if it is useful. For example, expose one population of users to a version of the application using a Green button, expose a similar population of users to a version of the application that uses a Blue button. The feedback from A/B testing compares the usage of these versions of the applications to determine which color button appears to make a difference in the usage of the application. This is one way of enriching the application development process itself.

Another example of enriching your data without additional data is migrating from simple metrics to a story. Creating an infographic from summaries of the data is a fantastic way to change how to use the data.

Each step in this process creates exponential knowledge enrichment. Enriching simple data into sophisticated stories and straightforward visuals will drive new questions, new requests for enrichment, and new ways of using the data.

One challenge of the endgame is helping personnel visualize and understand the resulting enriched data. Most humans easily process data in 2 dimensions, rows and columns. This is one of the main reasons Excel spreadsheets and CSV files are the tool of choice for exchanging data. Give someone a CSV file with meaningful headers, and this data can be loaded into Excel, Python, R, or just about any data processing tool or language. However, it's difficult for us to process more than two-dimensional data, such as bringing data together from multiple applications, relating it to each other using business keys, and elaborating on the definitions of the data by using semantic methods. Accurately representing this multidimensional data in some visualization that brings value to the business is its own unique challenge. Having colors represent dimensions, certain shapes represent different categories of items, and the space itself on the page to represent some other dimension enriches the data. Adding data from external data providers or collecting data from various knowledge graphs that make up the semantic web will provide additional details that may not have been considered before.

Self-service reporting

Suppose your organization has neither the dedicated knowledge workers to do its own analytics nor the budget to hire outside analysts. Self-service platforms such as Tableau and PowerBI enable non-developers to create data products, analysis, and reporting artifacts. Giving your business analysts access to tools supported by a good data team, whether they are called DataOps, or just data engineers, these self-service type tools can be an efficient way to get started looking at data with fresh eyes.

As we have seen, in application development, follow a process every time there is a need for an application to change. It can be followed quickly, of course, but it must be followed or threaten the stability of the environment. Self-service reporting allows for some separation of duties to allow the application development team to focus on their priorities while giving your business analysts the tools they need to produce reports independently and on their own schedule.

Using a dimensional data model as the foundation of a self-service reporting framework reduces the learning curve for creating new reports. Having an enriched set of dimensional tables, closely related to a set of fact tables creates an environment where reporting becomes a drag-and-drop exercise rather than a project to write new software.

With self-service reporting, a published set of data is available and documented in the data catalog, with access given via tools. From this starting point, an analyst, data scientist, or business user can drop data elements onto a screen, rearrange them till they have some meaning, publish this visualization for others to review, and then discuss the meaning of their findings with others.

Machine learning

Machine learning is where the value of your knowledge workers begins to become apparent. Using algorithms that learn from the data itself, provided the production quality data you are working with is available, machine learning processes identify patterns in the data using mathematical techniques. There are lots of books on machine learning, and this book will not cover many of the use cases that other literature has already clarified. One fine example is https://technicspub.com/machine-learning-and-data-science/.

The essence of machine learning is to apply an algorithm to a set of data and use the output of this algorithm to identify relationships, context, or similarity within the organic groups the data itself identifies. For example, if a customer purchases product X, there is an 88% probability that product Y will be purchased, there is a good chance that these two products are related. Regardless of what their names are, knowing this information is useful to most departments. Merchandising will want to ensure these two products are available in similar quantities. Marketing will want to include coupons for both products when they contact the customer, or they may want to place a sale on product X while ensuring that product Y is nearby. Finance will want to ensure that they purchase both products together. The specific use cases of knowing this information will vary depending on the business, but knowing this insight impacts the departments receiving these insights.

The most important step in any machine learning process is feature selection. Feature selection is the process where you automatically or manually select those features which contribute most to your prediction variable or output in which you are interested. This is an iterative process where features are tested. Then the algorithm is scored for accuracy in making predictions. Features are then either eliminated or enriched to improve the accuracy and reliability of the machine learning algorithm.

We will touch on the scientific process shortly, but each of these features needs to be related to the business problem being solved. As we have already discussed in gathering data from various sources and combining it into a solid Enrichment Platform, machine learning is one way to have all of this data from different sources brought together to add value to the organization The most important step in any machine learning process is feature selection. The most important step in any machine learning process is feature selection.

Feature selection

Finding out the importance of these features on your goal by using different machine learning algorithms will give you confidence that a pattern that has been identified is both real and important.

Independent machine learning algorithms should support each other. I worked on a problem once where I was using simple regression techniques to determine if the day of the week had an impact on sales. I found something interesting. I shared my findings with some of my co-workers, they told me they had done some different analysis using other mathematical techniques, but my findings were consistent with theirs. If a pattern exists in the data, even different approaches should identify similar patterns.

Identifying a pattern using regression on a data set is exciting. Taking that same set of data and applying a clustering algorithm should show you some similar results. This consensus of the machine learning models will give more confidence that the pattern identified is legitimate.

Advances are made by answering questions. Discoveries are made by questioning answers.

Bernard Haisch

Data science

Raw data provides no context and little insight, but enriched data is, well, rich with possibilities. The essence of data science is to extract meaning from enriched data by understanding the relationships, similarity, and context of our data. The goal of the enrichment process for data science is to provide as much relevant additional context to any kind of machine learning algorithm to make it useful. For example, is it pertinent to an analysis that it was raining the day a purchase was made?

Boiling down all this data into a set of mathematical expressions or equations is the most valuable step. This can be done with machine learning processes or deriving an actual set of mathematical terms showing a relationship between two or more sets of data.

Getting to the point where there is a set of dials that can be turned to adjust the momentum of the flywheel for the business, gives executives the ability to pivot the organization to meet the ever-changing needs of its customers.

Getting to the point where data science techniques are being applied to the same data that is represented through traditional business intelligence techniques enhances the entire enrichment process. A traditional report using self-service analytics or other business intelligence-type tools should support the findings of even a sophisticated data science model. Recall the earlier example where data scientists applied separate algorithms to identify if the day of the week impacted sales—using the same data, a business intelligence tool should show that that on the day of the week identified by the data science approach, sales would be different. So long as the data being used by the knowledge workers, business analysts, and data scientists is the same, the results will be the same.

Doing signal analysis on interaction data, then comparing those signals with traditional rows-and-columns analysis and reporting is one way of enriching the data you have. I did this with some interaction data for an online education platform. The waveforms could identify groups of users that we had not been able to identify using other means. When we took this same data that the waveforms had identified and did further analysis on those interactions, we were able to see consistent results in identifying this pattern. To elaborate, a "normal" waveform is just a curve that shows the shape of a wave at a given time. It will cycle up and down forever unless some outside influence is exerted.

The patterns we identified showed that each student's interactions showed some variance in this up and down cycle. In fact, we identified users that behaved similarly under various circumstances, and all achieved similar outcomes. We took these waveforms that each student produced and grouped them together using clustering analysis. These student cohorts all behaved similarly structurally, and these structural similarities all produced similar outcomes.

Not every scenario calls for a data scientist. In business, 80% of the data needed to answer business questions can be presented in a solid stable enriched data platform. Perhaps this number is even closer to 90%. The remaining 10-20% are fascinating questions that need sophisticated statistical methods like those used by a data scientist. However, that smaller percentage of the questions needs closer to 100% of the data. One example that comes to mind about using 100% of the data is in the healthcare space. Analyzing patient medical records looking for disease patterns limiting the data to 60 days' worth of data defeats the purpose of doing a full analysis looking for patterns of how certain diseases progress over time.

In one organization I worked with, our leadership talked a lot about using data science to make better decisions. However, the data science team did not have a clear communication pathway to the executive team. The goals of the project were more in tune with deploying a business intelligence solution to enable the vast majority of knowledge workers. None of the tools needed for proper machine learning were approved. All of the questions indicated the need for simply an enriched data platform that would allow the organization's knowledge workers to easily get enriched data in a stable manner.

For any data science, machine learning, forecasting, prediction, or artificial intelligence algorithm to work, you must have high-quality data. If the data used to test and verify an algorithm has a bias towards or against one type of person or another, then the algorithm's output will be biased. For example, if you are writing an algorithm to do voice recognition and only use a small sample size of one or two men, the algorithm may not recognize a woman. Likewise, if you use only native speakers to train the algorithm, then the algorithm may not understand people with non-native accents. Differing accents will influence the accuracy of the model. The data fed to the algorithm to train it was not sufficiently enriched to include enough samples.

The enrichment of our data to prevent built-in biases, preconceptions, or even discrimination is our responsibility as data experts. The knowledge workers can only work with the data they have available to them. Therefore, we must ensure they have the data necessary to prevent these types of biases.

Data science is one of the fastest growth areas for new tools and techniques in recent years. While each new tool can present a value-add to your enrichment and analytics processes, there is some risk to the stability of the enrichment platform. It may be valuable to replace one tool with another if it can be determined that the value of replacing an old tool will outweigh the benefit of continuing to use it. Regardless of whether it is desired or not, some due thought must be given to whether using a new tool will make things more efficient, cost-effective, or valuable. Some methods of measuring these metrics need to be adopted before any new tools are adopted.

In the philosophic sense, observation shows and experiment teaches.

Claude Bernard

The scientific method

We are hopefully all familiar with the scientific method from our high school science classes. In essence, it is a process for ascertaining whether certain hypotheses (guesses) about the world are true. But what does it have to do with data? In short, data is the evidence on which the scientific method depends. Richard Feynman illustrates this well when he explains how to use data to test an algorithm:

Now I'm going to discuss how we would look for a new law. In general, we look for a new law by the following process. First, we guess it. (Audience laughter) No, don't laugh, that's the truth. Then we compute the consequences of the guess, to see what, if this is right, if this law we guess is right, to see what it would imply and then we compare the computation results to nature or we say compare to experiment or experience, compare it directly with observations to see if it works.

If [your guess] disagrees with experiment, it's wrong. In that simple statement is the key to science. It doesn't make any difference how beautiful your guess is, it doesn't matter how smart you are, who made the guess, or what his name is ... If it disagrees with experiment, it's wrong. That's all there is to it.

Richard Feynman

Answering the most important questions of our enterprise is the main reason we are collecting and enriching all this data. The scientific method shows us how to use our data to answer those questions and drive us forward.

The Scientific Method is the most profound invention in the history of all mankind. It should be embraced and relied on throughout all organizations that make decisions based on data.

With this method, the Art of Discovery can become a repeatable scientific process. Of course, there are still opportunities for stumbling upon a great discovery, but the Method wraps the stumble into the gait of reliability. No longer is mankind limited to myths, stories, hunches, or gut feelings to explain things.

Many visualizations of the scientific method portray it as a linear set of progressions. You do step 1, then move on to step 2, and so on. However, I prefer to visualize it as a cycle. Each part of the process can lead to other steps. At any one point in the process, you can begin with the other steps to confirm your findings. During analysis of a set of data, there have been plenty of times that more questions were found that subsequently led to further insights.

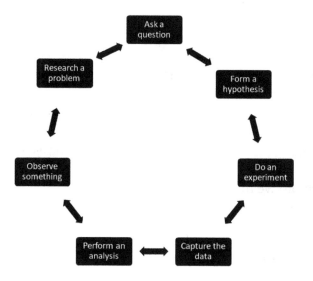

Each step in the cycle is closely related to all the others. That means we need to keep all of the core principles in mind as our enriched data leads to further use of the data. Likewise, understanding how the various aspects of the scientific method fit together solidifies the business cases for the strategy employed to solve problems.

In producing a piece of analysis following the principles of the scientific method, it is important to show your work. It could be as simple as producing a document that has an outline similar to the structure below:

We observed this behavior.

We did the following research by looking at this or that data.

The question that occurred to us to summarize this observation is this.

We formed this hypothesis to answer the question.

We did the following experiments.

This is the data we gathered related to the experiment.

The analysis performed indicates this hypothesis is correct.

Therefore we make this recommendation.

Observation

Observations are memorable.

Seeing the same reports, dashboards, or visualizations day in and day out can become tedious for many knowledge workers. But having a set of standard reports that show the same metrics each day makes it easy to identify when something about the data has made a significant change. If you have looked at the same types of reports on your screen every day for some period of time, and you notice something different, you will remember that something odd happened that day. Even if it is not a bump in a line on a chart, if suddenly you realize while looking at two dashboards that there is some relationship you had not noticed before you will remember that moment. You will start to understand this relationship and be able to point back to that observation.

When something does appear odd, the knowledge worker can review the data flows, verify the data itself, and speak to the application administrator to confirm the data is accurate. Perhaps the data needs some additional enrichment. Or it could be something important that needs to be brought to someone else's attention. Sometimes an observation is an insight that could have a profound effect on what you are working on. For example, suppose you get an unusually high number of complaints from customers saying they cannot find items using a search capacity within your application. In any case, it's time for the knowledge worker to do some research.

Research

Research takes time.

Research may be something as simple as researching a particular machine learning technique or researching the trends of a supplier over time. However, research requires time to complete.

Sometimes the research is as straightforward as looking at existing data. Sometimes certain users need to be surveyed. Bringing the results of these surveys back to a consolidated data platform and keeping the survey results available over time allows the knowledge worker to see the changes in opinions over time. If the data is already enriched before the need for research comes up, the knowledge worker's job is much easier.

Receiving complaints about search results in your application could mean that some knowledge workers need to research the search capabilities within the application. Are search criteria captured? Do we have the data to identify what all users are searching for, and what result is provided to them through the user interface?

All of the pieces come together in research.

- Who entered this data? (Data Access).

- What is the definition for this data element? (Data Dictionary)

- Where did the data come from? (Data Lineage)

- How was this data captured, and why did the user enter this data? (Business Rules)

- Why did the user enter this data? (Business Rules)

Once you have all this contextual information, doing research is straightforward. Knowing that the data used to do research is stable, reliable, accessible, and has a clear lineage provides trust in the researcher's mind.

This should be as simple as reviewing the data dictionary for where the search criteria are stored. It may be in applications logs that are stored in a different structure, location, and require different access. If this is not already built into the data pipelines, this will require a whole project to acquire the data and make it available for analysis.

A researcher can create as well as consume information. For example, a knowledge worker might group users into cohorts and follow these cohorts through their customer experience. This is a valuable research project in confirming or giving counterarguments for the requirements of application usage. That new information they create enriches the data that has already been collected and creates new data as part of their experiments, analysis, and categorizations of data. That is not a primary objective of research, but it is a valuable side benefit.

Sometimes research involves the duplication of other studies applying your data to the analysis technique. For example, in one problem domain I was researching, we were having several difficulties identifying website user behaviors related to a particular outcome.

I found some studies where a waveform analysis technique was performed on a similar problem. I duplicated the research to ensure that I understood the technique and the raw data used. Then I replaced the data used in the documented experiments with some of our data. The outcome of this little research had similar results to the documented study. Expanding my research, I took more of our data and munged the data into the structure the algorithm was expecting. Again, the outcome gave me consistent results. I was able to feed into the next step of the analysis to identify cohorts of users that exhibited similar behavior. While this was something of a roundabout way to get to the solution, we were able to identify groups of students who exhibited similar behavior could have similar outcomes. It was the answer for which we had been searching.

This may seem like a roundabout way of solving a problem, but researching new techniques gave my team a new analytical tool in looking at consumer behavior. Within weeks, members of the team were talking about how to categorize various waveforms and what these similar waveforms meant for our outcomes expectations.

Question

Questions must be meaningful.

In World War II, the military came to the Strategic Research Group (SRG) with a problem. Planes needed to survive being shot but armoring too much of the plane would make it difficult to fly. So they brought some data to the SRG and asked the question: Based on these bullet hole patterns, where should we add more armor to the planes? Abraham Wald, one of the senior statisticians on the team changed the question. The question became, what happened to the planes that had holes in different parts of the plane? They did not return; therefore, the armor does not go where the bullet holes are. It goes where the bullet holes are not. On the Engines. Wald was able to rightly surmise that the planes that had not returned had bullet holes that were not represented in the data. Those planes had been shot down. So, the planes that had survived and returned could continue to fly even with holes. (https://medium.com/the-innovation/the-missing-bullet-holes-and-abraham-wald-25e68d7a870f n.d.)

Most data scientists today are not faced with such life and death type questions. However, the spirit of asking the right question remains.

There is an art to creating meaningful questions. Your questions must be testable and specific, and they should avoid opinions and unfounded assumptions.

Some excellent questions can be answered with simple, measurable data. For example, "What time of day do we see the most customers?" This question is easy to answer with a rich time dimension on your reporting system.

Take a question like, "Why are users bored when they are using our application?" This assumes that users are bored.

It also assumes the level of excitement a user has is meaningful to their use of the application. It further assumes that we can measure the level of excitement that a user possesses. While these may be interesting questions, their answers can't be quantified, measured, tested against, and used to improve interactions between the user and our application.

A better question for the data scientist is: "What is the level of engagement do users exhibit when using our application?" This is a question we can answer programmatically. If a user logs into a shopping app, checks one or two things, then logs out, that engagement score may be low. If a user logs in, orders many items, and then checks out using their shopping cart, that engagement score may be intermediate or high. Other questions might include, "Did the user search for things they could not find? If this happened, did the user search for something similar or log out?" These are all types of things that could be used to score a user's engagement for our application. Scoring your users then, aggregating that data to show how many users fit into each engagement score grouping, could be very useful.

Hypothesis

The hypothesis is a guess that answers the question. We test the hypothesis using data to see if it is true or false.

"We need more data to support our hypothesis." While this may work for Television police detectives, this approach should be discouraged in the real world. We never want to assume the truth of our hypothesis and search for data to support it. Instead, we want to let the data guide us to finding out whether the hypothesis is true or false.

Using our previous example, we could create a hypothesis: Users who find items in their search results tend to buy more items. This is a hypothesis that could be tested. Gather the data together, review search results, compare this with the size of the shopping carts for the same session as users that performed searches, and you can determine if the hypothesis is true or false.

Experiment

Experiments stress the Hypothesis.

One of my mother's favorite sayings was, "Do something, even if it is wrong."

We have a solid question and a hypothesis that may provide the answer to the question. Now it is time to run an experiment. In the search example from the previous section, we can look at historical trends to identify users that searched for items. Create multiple groups of users, those that found what they were searching for and their purchase patterns. Then have a separate group of users that did not find what they were looking for and their purchase patterns. Are the expected results the same between the two groups? While this is an observational experiment, it will provide some statistical meaning. This puts some numerical stress on the proposed answer from the hypothesis. Either there is support for this hypothesis, or there is none.

Even if the Hypothesis is wrong, the experiment should stress the hypothesis enough to show whether it is wrong or not.

The important statistical modeling should take place in the mind of the analyst, not in the computer. While I have used the term model many times throughout this book, when referring to a model, I am referring to a mathematical model that gives a valid explanation of the data. When dealing with observational data, some method of randomization of the samples is needed to ensure that all cases are exposed to the model. In active experimentation when dealing with users online over time, the nature of the experiments done in data science is double-blind. The person running the experiment should not know the person exposed to the experiment; likewise the participant in the experiment should not know that an experiment is being conducted.

All data generated by the experiment should be captured and used as an additional enrichment source for the raw data. Analysis is done and summarized for producing the findings of the experiment, but the raw data should be captured and the same experiments should be repeated periodically to determine the changes in behavior that occur over time.

An experiment is not working software—it is a test that produces data. It has been said that the big tech companies do many experiments simultaneously. This can only be accomplished by many things being stable and offering a few multiple choices for the experiment. Dual experiments can be run simultaneously so long as their expected outcomes have no direct relationship with each other.

An experiment should be repeated an odd number of times to ensure that the results could be interpreted as statistically significant. Ideally, each experiment will produce results consistent with the expected outcome. If the expected outcome of an experiment is either yes or no, which it generally should be, running the experiments only an even number of times may not specifically identify a pattern.

I have heard of many predictive models related to consumer behavior built on data before the outbreak of Covid-19 that simply had no predictive value during the pandemic itself. However, constant experimentation of consumer behavior, choices, and consumption patterns will provide valuable input to making business decisions as the world continues to adjust to the pandemic's impact on our collective behavior.

Data

Data must be of good quality to be useful to the experimentation process.

Data lineage becomes more important as the data migrates to other systems away from the original application that captured the data. Knowing where the data came from, what transformations were done to the data, and how frequently the data is copied are all critical components to data lineage. Why are any transformations needed to the data?

Further, we must ask if the data usable for enrichment. Does the data need to be adjusted in any way? Are the values expected, and can the data from one system be matched to another system?

As an example of data quality, let me use my own name as an example: Is Doug Needham the same as Douglas Needham? Does one system use a middle name or middle initial while another one does not? If you allow nulls in one field like middle name, and that data needs to be combined into a full name field how are the nulls translated? Data quality will impact any analysis that needs to be done.

In one analysis I was working on, we noticed an extremely high value for one particular field coming from our customer support application. When we did some investigation, we discovered that the field was the first option on a screen for customer service agents to select a reason for a customer not wanting further information. When the customer did not provide a reason, the data entry personnel just chose the first option. We had to adjust the application to modify this option to mean "No reason provided" rather than the default, which was "Dissatisfied with product."

New data is constantly coming in, and any analysis, recommendation, or forecast should be based on the most current data. A subsequent analysis, recommendation, or forecast could negate the prior results. It is vital for the confidence in the knowledge worker that it is obvious what data is most current versus what data is weeks or even months old. One recommendation provided based on yesterday's data will not be as useful as a recommendation provided based on today's data (again, think about how the pandemic changed consumer behavior). Likewise, a recommendation given in a few weeks will be even more valuable as a situation is changing over time.

The knowledge worker is dependent on the accuracy of the enrichment platform, and there are those that are dependent on the recommendation of the knowledge worker. The knowledge worker's confidence in their recommendations is directly related to their confidence in the accuracy, quality, and validity of the data in the enrichment platform.

In addition to data quality, the personnel working on the data must have the required skillset. When putting together an analytics team, every team member has the expertise that contributes to the organization's confidence in the recommendations coming from the enrichment platform.

Having all the required quality controls mentioned previously related to statistical process control for the flow of data becomes critical when recommendations need to be made that will impact many people for a long time.

Data is permanent. However, data should not reside in one data storage system for all time.

Taking data from its primary application, enriching it, and transforming the data structure to make for more efficient use of reporting and analytics makes managing a data infrastructure so much more efficient.

During the Enrichment phase, data can grow exponentially as new metrics are created from the basic data that is captured within the application.

Experiments run against the data actually generate more data about this data set. Storing all of this away from the primary application is the most well-thought-out solution to the problem of data storage.

Since we are talking about data permanence, I would be remiss to mention that periodically performing restores of any database backups you have taken is a best practice. Doing this verifies the media of the backup itself and ensures the DataOps team is well-practiced in case the need ever arises where it must be done while customers are waiting on the application to be back available.

Analysis

Analysis is repeatable.

Any finding by one knowledge worker documents their process and the data they use can be replicated by any other knowledge worker. This repeatability factor is crucial in making something adhere to scientific principles. If it can't be repeated, then it can't be modeled or experimented with.

Earlier I presented an example about doing an analysis on how the days of the week affected sales. Other people were able to come up with similar results using different analysis techniques. This is one way in which analysis is repeatable. Any analysis on the same data should produce similar results. The findings of the analysis should always be similar.

This is the principle behind peer review. Peer review is evaluating the work as a whole by one or more people with similar competencies as the producers of the work. This is necessary for a conclusion to be considered valid.

A knowledge worker will do some analysis. Then other knowledge workers should review those results. The second knowledge worker will ask questions such as "What were the assumptions? Where did the data come from? What was the hypothesis? How many experiments were run? What question was being answered?" The code or other process that produces the analysis is also reviewed to ensure it contains no embedded assumptions or biases.

These are part of the peer review process, especially when the analysis results in significant changes that will affect the entire business. This peer-review process has to be done for every meaningful analysis that is driving a change within an organization.

One way of peer-reviewing data analysis is through notebook technology. With a notebook, you can write a document containing live code, equations, visualizations, and narrative text and share it with others. Sharing these documents with other analysts allows them to see the data and the process for any analysis done. They can re-run the notebook using the same data. They can then verify the results by tweaking parts of the analysis done.

While analysis must be repeatable, the analysis results can change over time as new information is provided. Analysis is repeatable in that experts in their field can accurately reproduce an analysis given the same data. As new data comes in, those same experts can make new recommendations. For example, in the early days of a marketing campaign, one analysis may indicate that one type of demographic is the largest consumer of a given product. That same analysis done several weeks later with additional information could show that another demographic is the largest consumer of that same product. Although neither analysis is wrong, they are both accurate at the time of the analysis with the data given at the time. This is why for an enrichment platform to continue to be considered reliable, the date of the analysis along with the data captured for the analysis should be documented clearly.

The trusted advisor can certainly change their recommendations based on new evidence with no loss of credibility, so long as the advisor is confident with the data they have at the time of their recommendations.

Summary

The Data must flow to increase its value. Even if it is simply re-arranging the data within its original application into new structures that are better optimized for different use-cases than what was originally designed. Moving data from a set of applications to an enrichment platform like a data warehouse, operational data store, or a data lake increases its value and reduces the workload on the original systems.

Once the data starts flowing, it must be monitored closely by dedicated operations teams whose mission is to ensure that the movement of the data is done in a stable and repeatable approach.

Choosing what type of Enrichment Platform meets the needs of an organization is a strategic decision. Identifying things that can be done in an Enrichment Platform outside the application space will justify leaping from an application-centered enterprise to a data-first organization.

CHAPTER 5

Strategy

Plans are worthless, but planning is everything.

Dwight D. Eisenhower

The stage is set; all of the pieces are in place. The enrichment services team knows what data is available, where this data is stored, who has access to the data, and how the data from one application relates to data in another application.

What now? What problem are you trying to solve? These questions are all part of the enrichment decision process. Every team member should reasonably articulate how their work relates to the overall strategy outlined in the enrichment decision. And in turn, solving those problems should fit into your organization's overall mission and goals.

The power of the imagination is the only limit in the strategy of achieving an enriched services platform.

Data governance guides how to use the data, who can use the data for what purpose, and how the data is related to each other. Governance should also provide guidance for what data can and should be enriched, who should access the enriched data, and how the enriched data can support the business.

The things I've described all sound like a lot of work. But let me give some examples of how enriching data led me to looking at data in new ways to solve some problems.

Examples

In this section, I will bring all of these pieces together to demonstrate how enriching data meets the needs of the business.

Detecting anomalies

To identify an anomaly, you must first identify what is "typical" behavior. For one IoT solution I worked on, we were tasked with finding anomalies with connected devices to our network. IoT devices are supposed to only use a tiny bit of network bandwidth. The little SIM card placed in an IoT device is similar to the SIM card you have in your phone. We found out some of our users took the SIM card out of their devices and placed them in tablets to watch movies. This caused the bandwidth costs for our customers to go up. So we first looked at the "normal" behavior of the devices, then began looking for things that were not "normal."

The solution we arrived at based on the patterns we saw in the data was to reduce each device down to the waveform it generated through time. For example, some devices frequently put data on the network, some infrequently, and some were quite talkative.

We created a signal profile based on the device and the company type that the device belonged to.

By enriching the data the device was generating and categorizing that device profile by the company type, we were able to identify "typical" behavior for any device associated with that company.

This type of enrichment required data from multiple systems, our network infrastructure, our applications that related the devices to companies, and our salesforce system, which categorized each company into a type of business.

By consolidating these diverse data sources and enriching the low-level atomic data, we were able to identify the behaviors of the devices with reasonable accuracy. With very high accuracy, we were able to identify devices that were behaving abnormally, saving our customers bandwidth costs.

Identifying similar items

Our brains have evolved over millions of years to recognize similarity. We use things like size, shape, color, texture, volume, space, and time to name just a few. Sometimes our brains even identify patterns that don't exist, like seeing images in the clouds, our soup, or a slice of bread. In a business, identifying similar items is useful because we may want to recommend to our customers a similar product if the one they are looking for is not available. Netflix does this type of thing daily based on your viewing habits. For example, you may like this movie since you watched this other movie similar to this one.

Computers use enriched data to find similarities and patterns more accurately than our minds can on their own. One of my favorite tools for identifying similar items is to use graph techniques to identify similar items.

A well-defined graph structure breaks items down to their component parts and then creates a large graph to rapidly identify similar items. This is where graph databases excel.

I created a graph structure for a company in one use case, then populated the graph with all of the basic item data and several other categorical type data. As a result, we instantly identified items that were similar to the original item being considered. This required collecting non-obvious data about the items: people associated with it, various textual descriptions of the items, industry categorizations about the items, as well as naturally organic information about the items.

By preparing the data to identify the nodes and relationships before loading the data into a graph database, we were able to use the natural performance of the graph database to identify these items based on their similarity without pre-calculating similarity metrics.

The similarity metrics came out of the graph engine with the result of a simple query. This process saved weeks of engineering effort to perform advanced calculations to identify similar items.

Identifying most important influences

In many ways, enriching data is about adding new levels of categorical descriptions of numerical or measurement data. By doing this, you create new ways of looking at your data. When your knowledge workers have more perspectives to understand your applications' numerical and measurement data, they can bring more value to your organization.

A decision tree or classification tree uses measurement data to identify categories. More specifically, classification trees identify thresholds for various measurement data to identify which category some important outcome fits into.

In one analysis, I was requested to identify the most important factor in identifying students that may be at risk of dropping a course. We gathered outcome data from one system, and interaction data from all of the other applications where users performed interactions.

We created decision tree models using the known outcome and all of the other interaction data to identify the top three actions that users performed with similar outcomes. There were a few decision tree models we had to create based on some high-level categories. Still, once we did this, we were able to provide clear answers to identify the top three levels of interactions broken down by category that had the desired outcome. For example, students that interacted with us frequently were not at risk, and students that had high levels of interactions with us during the first four weeks of a class were less likely to drop out of the course.

When we identified users who were underperforming in their interactions based on this model, these users could be nudged to prevent students from dropping the course.

Since these users were using our platform to achieve these outcomes, these nudges were designed to help them understand what they needed to do to achieve their desired outcomes.

Implementation

There is a common representation in the data industry that illustrates why one would want to enrich data. The Knowledge Pyramid (Wikimedia Commons, by Longlivetheux, CC-BY-SA) represents the relationship between Data, Information, Knowledge, and Wisdom.

Just capturing and storing data alone does little to progress data towards knowledge.

Data itself is a raw building block of the pyramid. Enriching data with other data creates information. Deriving information from the data by enriching the data with context generates knowledge. Relating information to other information and testing whether this will help us accomplish something generates knowledge. Wisdom is in discerning how to use that knowledge to solve a problem, understand behavior, or change processes.

Let's work through a simple example about a business that runs multiple bars throughout the country.

Data: A customer buys three pitchers of beer on Saturday in one of our bars.

Information: This customer, along with several others, buys three pitchers of beer every few days.

Knowledge: Multiple customers come in every few days and split the order such that one person buys beer while others pay for appetizers.

Wisdom: Customers come into the bar during baseball games played by the local team. We need to have adequate supplies and staffing during game time.

This particular example may seem obvious. However, it is the non-obvious patterns that require an enrichment process to see.

Lightly enrich data

This is the place where I would say most organizations stay. They enrich data from one application with data from another application to identify key performance indicators for the business. They combine this with some sophisticated date and time dimensions to roll up data based on Gregorian, fiscal, and other calendars, then show data aggregated by various time periods.

This is a useful start, but there may be some more nuggets of information within your data space that have not been realized: Have you recently calculated a customer's lifetime value? Which applications have higher customer value?

These can be calculated straightforwardly by combining key data from all your applications into a well-thought-out data warehouse environment.

Enrich some data

Enriching some data is a step towards enriching as much data as possible. Identify gaps in knowledge about your data. For example, would it be more helpful to understand customer demographics? This data may be in an application already, but have the demographics themselves been studied, grouped, segmented, and classified? Are these classifications groups rolled back into the application? Can the application space even use these classifications? How groups of customers use your products is valuable information to your marketing team.

Enrich as much data as possible

The more data you enrich, the more options are available for driving new opportunities. These opportunities could be for new customers, new products, or even eliminating applications, services, and other cost centers that may not be living up to expectations.

Creating an enrichment services team with its own set of priorities independent of any frontline application development process, and provides insights to the knowledge workers and leadership team, will give leadership the tools it needs to make well thought-out decisions for the betterment of the organization.

Summary

Strategy is a choice. There will be a cost regardless of the decision. Making the decision not to officially create an Enrichment Platform only means that small pockets of tiny enrichment platforms are created by the various business teams that need the data to be enriched.

The complexity of the environment is only increased by ignoring the needs of the enterprise to have a stable Enrichment Platform.

To migrate from an application focus to a data-first strategy requires some due thought to make the right decision.

In keeping with the stair-step analogy I have used before, I strongly suggest building a smaller prototype enrichment platform, then iterate changes thoughtfully to grow the Enrichment Platform. Taking these steps transparently with open communication throughout your organization allows the data leader to share the successes and communicate effectively when there are failures.

Transparent leadership that learns both from success and failures engenders trust with peers in any organization.

Taking these steps to create the Enriched Enterprise will transform any organization into a Data First organization.

CHAPTER 6

The Enriched Enterprise

No man is an island entire of itself; every man is a piece of the continent, a part of the main; if a clod be washed away by the sea, Europe is the less, as well as if a promontory were, as well as any manner of thy friends or of thine own were; any man's death diminishes me, because I am involved in mankind.

John Donne

When Richard Douglas Fosbury set out to be a high jumper, he did not develop a new technique immediately. Instead, he followed the footsteps of others until there was a reason not to follow them. So how do you know if *you* need to abandon your old techniques in favor of ones laid out here?

This is a lot of work to collect this information about the data, create pipelines, monitor the pipelines, and create whole new ecosystems for how an organization's data is used. Enrichment drives insights. Insight drives innovation. When you change the way you look at data, you change the value you can get from it.

As with any game, there is a decision to even play the game before it has begun. This decision can be explicit or implicit.

Some games you actively decide to participate in, like the baseball game at the company picnic. Then, you decide whether the fun and camaraderie you will enjoy playing the game are worth the soreness and possible injuries.

Some games you play whether you know it or not! By accepting the terms and conditions of applications you choose to use on your mobile device, you participate in someone else's enrichment game. You provide the data points with which they make decisions, including whether to advertise to you, send you an email, or show you a way to increase your available lives in Candy Crush.

It is important to make a well-informed decision when deciding to play the enrichment game. This game can be quite valuable to your organization. However, some costs and tradeoffs come with playing. There will be additional costs in time, resources, computing capabilities, and the number of dedicated full-time personnel to make the game successful and worth the effort.

This is a long game, and it's a team sport. It should not be entered into lightly. Give it the resources to succeed: training, new hires, dedicated resources looking at data flows, ETL processes, and peer-reviewed analysis. It could bring new value to your organization. But without the decision processes put in place above and communicated effectively to the whole organization, it will be a game destined to fail. Below are some questions you need to ask yourself about the project's viability for your organization.

Are you ready?

Are you the right person to play the Enrichment Game? Finding one individual with all the skills noted throughout this book would be rare indeed. However, one person can identify the needs for these things and verify their existence. Once all the pieces are identified and brought together, a team must pull the data from the source applications. This team is the foundation of the DataOps team that will monitor and stabilize this environment for the duration of the life of the Enrichment Services.

This is not a project where a team can be formed, work on a few things, and then work on other projects. Instead, this team will be the foundation of how data that is to be enriched moves throughout the organization.

Are your customers ready?

The terms and conditions for any customer-facing application should be specific enough to say that any data collected by the application will be used for enrichment and aggregation, yet vague enough to allow for the advances in technology that will come about through the life of the business.

Data breaches are a common occurrence making headlines quite frequently. Customers are becoming more aware of the volume of data that many organizations collect, store, and use. They want to be reassured that all use cases of their data are protected and conform to the terms and conditions they agree to when signing up to use your services.

Enriching the company's data to provide better services and offerings may not make up for a data breach where their enriched data is open for all to see. However, each enrichment use case must adhere to overall company data governance guidelines and principles to protect the data.

Is your organization ready?

The three things that are absolutely necessary for the success of an Enrichment project are strong leadership, data governance, and a dedicated data engineering team. Think of each of these three things similarly to the three things needed for a fire: fuel, heat, and oxygen. Each of these things is needed for a fire to burn—remove any one of them and the fire will fizzle out. Likewise, if you have a dedicated data engineering team and strong data governance with no strong leadership, there is no direction for the enrichment services team to go. When having strong leadership and good data governance with no data engineering team, things will get implemented only when other business priorities allow time to do things with data. Hint: this will never happen.

Having strong leadership that is recognized and part of the overall conversations involved in defining and setting the strategy of the business and the workload is the most important critical success factors in getting the Enriched Data Platform adopted, refined, and available for the organizations knowledge workers to give a voice to your data.

Playing this game begins with clear leadership and accountability. Accountability, responsibility, and authority for the enrichment of corporate data are the three-legged stool that all this is built upon.

Who ultimately has the authority, responsibility and authority to ensure that all of the pieces are maintained, available and integrated to the processes throughout the organization?

Probably the Chief Data Officer, of course. Not all organizations have a CDO. Someone with the blessings of the various executives needs to hold the reins for ensuring these various pieces are recognized as important and become useful for all the various teams outside the data organization.

Peter Drucker once said, "Culture eats strategy for breakfast." The culture of your company will determine success regardless of how effective your strategy may be. If your company's culture requires drastic changes to focus on Data Strategy, creating a robust set of Enrichment Services, and using that enriched data to improve your organization will be more difficult.

In a large enterprise, the connectedness of all applications could look like this:

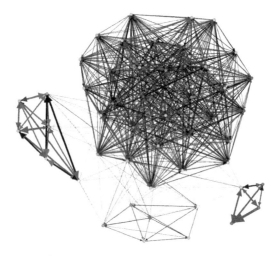

In this graph, each dot is an application system. Each line shows a data flow between the two systems. This is a Graph theory approach to looking at an Enterprise Architecture. A DataOps team manages each of the data flows. If there are any issues with any of these connections, they must be resolved quickly for the data to flow and meet the needs of the dependent application. For example, a core set of applications exchange lots of data, and then through mergers and acquisitions, other applications are brought into the enterprise and data is exchanged with them.

How does this fit into business strategy?

Let's talk about the decision processes involved in creating an enrichment platform. This is more than just a data warehouse. There are techniques available to take raw data in various forms, do some processing, and then create new enriched artifacts to assist in decision-making.

The process of creating the Enrichment Platform should closely tie to the Business Strategy. If the larger Business strategy is too generic and not focused enough, then choosing some part of the business strategy that the Enrichment Platform will support first is the best first step. Once that first step is built, it becomes easier to set the priorities for which step should be the follow-on step. Each step in the process should be categorized as doing the next right thing.

- What is the relationship of the enrichment project to corporate strategy?

- o Is it directly or indirectly supporting strategy? For example, are you creating a product to sell? Which of these overall goals will the enrichment project support: Increase stability, reduce cost, or increase efficiency?

- What is the data provider?
  - o Is it an application, the logs of an application, social media, a data broker, a statistical provider, or a government entity? If it is a government entity, which government?

- Which departments are affected by the enrichment project?
  - o Will those departments get some value returned in how they see data?

- Where in the customer journey are insights expected?
  - o If one of the initiatives of the enrichment project is related to the customer journey, where in their journey is data collected? How will it be enriched? Will the customer gain value from this effort directly or indirectly?

- What is the type of data that will either be enriched or provide enrichment?

- o Text, survey data, relational, application data, third-party API data will have to be conformed in some way to show the relationship with the data to be enriched.

- What are the legal implications of using this data?
  - o Do the terms and conditions users agree to allow the use of this data for enrichment purposes? Can the data you want to use for enrichment be stored within your country's borders? How long is this data allowed to be used? How will that affect the enrichment process if a user wants you to remove all of their personal data?

- What is the raw cost of acquisition?
  - o If this is a third party, what is the cost of the data? What is the cost of time and person-hours necessary to acquire, manipulate, store, and conform the data to fit into the enrichment platform?

- What is the cost of integration?
  - o Will there be a storage cost? How many people will be involved in this integration project?

- What is the estimated value?
  - o Does this estimated value outweigh the overall costs in time, energy, and value that

your   resources   have   already   been committed to?

- What are the expectations of the knowledge worker?
    - The knowledge worker will gain new data available to them. Are they aware of how this data affects previous analysis and other data products?

There is immediate feedback for any decision made in many games: you can tell whether the ball went through the hoop only seconds after taking the shot. However, in the Enrichment Game, you need a degree of patience in knowing if the right move has been made. Setting clear expectations of value early in the process will provide the groundwork for knowing when the expected value can be realized.

Ultimately the creation of an Enriched Services Production area should be judged by capabilities. Therefore, the question to be answered that provides the most insight into whether your enrichment platform is successful or not should be:

What can we do now that we could not do before?

CHAPTER 7

Play the Game!

Creating an enterprise prepared to play the enrichment game is important to differentiate between a project and a program. A project has a beginning, middle, and end. A project accomplishes a specific goal. When that goal is met, people move on to the next project. The Enrichment Game is a program. It is constantly being played. Data is constantly moving, and there is no end to this until the business goes under. So let's take a look at the "big picture" of what it takes to bring all these pieces together to play the game.

Today is your first day as the Chief Data Officer at ACTA Corp. You have met with the board of directors and the CEO. You have been tasked with creating an enriched data platform that allows the executive team and their knowledge workers visibility into all of the applications throughout the organization. What do you do?

1. Identify the data available.
2. Create a data operations team.
3. Enrich the data to provide additional value.

First, you have to know where the data is and what data is collected in every application. This is the Data Catalog. Simply gather the data dictionaries of every application into a single location.

Second, create a data operations team that will bring all the data that reflects the organization's key performance metrics into a single location. This data operations team needs access to all application data regardless of what type of database the application is using.

Third, enrich the data. How do you identify what opportunities exist for enriching data? Speak to the people who are currently working with the data already available. Find the people in the organization that work with daily reports. Ask them what other perspectives would make the data more valuable. This feedback will give you guidance on what gaps exist to make the data better. Getting to know the people working with the data already and what problems they have encountered will be the guiding light in enriching the data to make the data more valuable for them and help them show the value of the data to the organization.

Since some of your applications involve credit processing, the external data brokers' data needs to be brought together into this enrichment platform to show how effective the creditworthiness of consumers is affecting the company's bottom line.

Can all this be done within the next ninety days? Do you have all the tools needed at your disposal? How do the application priorities of meeting their needs agree with your priorities of gathering data together?

Knowing that all of these pieces need to come together efficiently and stably, are you confident that your goals are achievable? Does everyone in the organization understand how your goals will end up helping them achieve their goals? To bring everyone and everything together to accomplish this, your strategy needs to consider all of the pieces, players, and rules that every team within the organization is following.

The rules that need to be put into place for moving data around must be consistent with the already familiar rules. Once you have everything together, are your knowledge workers sophisticated enough to start making forecasts and predictions about segments of consumers?

To not only play the enrichment game, but to win it, there are things you need to have and to understand.

- A rich data dictionary.
- Teams monitoring data flows.
- External data providers.
- A well-documented and enriched data repository.
- Proper analytical tools with access to the data repository.

- Knowledge workers whose familiarity with the business allows them to answer most questions themselves.
- Knowledge workers capable of making forecasts and predictions.
- Ways of checking the validity of the forecasts.
- The ability to pivot quickly depending on the outcome of the forecasts.

As with any game, you must play the hand you are dealt. There will be times coming into a new organization where few of these pieces, players, and processes exist. Worse yet, they may have a similar name, yet none of the thing's characteristics are needed. One of the worst organizations I worked with had a C-level executive who correctly used many of these words yet did not understand how everything fit together to accomplish something new.

While the options are limited, the process is the same. You have to build these things as you go, to ultimately have things like a data catalog, data operations team, well-documented data models, repeatable processes, and trained knowledge workers. The dependencies do not change. Each step builds on the prior step, and the foundational components are necessary to be stable and working for any of the later components to work properly.

Each step of the Enrichment Game requires some stability and some agility. Stabilize things, monitor and improve them, then make agile adjustments. The Game itself is ongoing and needs constant attention, adjustment, and tweaking. However, it must be reliable. I have seen data operations teams treated as development teams, and the organization has suffered. When there is a production problem, it cannot wait for a backlog to be cleared to fix it. The Knowledge workers rely on the stability of the environment to answer the questions posed to them.

A data engineering team with strong leadership can implement some interesting things. Still, with no data governance, the data engineering team will spend all of its time cleaning and conforming data to facilitate knowledge workers and data visualization experts. They will constantly be fixing things that are broken rather than proactively working with leadership to identify important trends, patterns, and cohorts needed to drive the overall business decision-making process.

No matter your level of experience with these tools, techniques, and approaches for gathering data together, you must play the game.

A deeper understanding of your business and your customers comes from enriching the data within your enterprise.

Look at consolidated data in new ways.

Learn from the data, and understand what the data represents.

Experiment, pivot, but above all, enrich the data you have available. Because if you don't do it, someone else will. And that someone else may be your competitor.

Our goal is to grow our business. That only comes by a thorough understanding of your data and what it represents. In many ways, business is like the game of poker. Our competitors sit across the table from us, our customers are the cards we are dealt. Every critical decision that is made depends on the cards we have in our hand at the time. Each of these cards have no markings on them originally. So the value of our hand entirely depends on the value of each card.

The only way we know the value of each card is to enrich those individual transactions that occur as our customers interact with us with the best contextual information we can find. Understanding the lifetime value of each customer, what those customers' demographics are, their buying patterns, and how they see us as valuable makes our hands more valuable than the hands of our competitors.

Play the Game.

Enrich your data.

CHAPTER 8

Further Reading

This book has given an overview of several highly complex concepts so that you can see how they all fit together. However, for more in-depth information, I recommend the following.

In my book *Data Structure Graphs* (Needham 2015), I describe how you can think of each application system as a vertex in a graph and all of the various data transfers as edges.

There are frameworks and guidelines for all of the above mentioned. I would encourage the reader to explore *The Data Management Body of Knowledge* (DMBOK) (DAMA International 2017), and *The Cross-Industry Standard Process for Data Mining* (CRISP-DM) (Blokdyk 2018) to understand some background information put together by people that work with data exclusively.

The DMBOK is a collection of definitions, explanations, and clarifications for the data professional. It encapsulates the knowledge of many data practitioners and codifies the terminology used by masters of the art of data administration. Using this as a reference for building an enrichment platform will clarify terminology regardless of your business domain. When working with vendors, analytics providers, or other third parties, having the DMBOK will be a useful touchpoint to clarify the needs for building an enrichment platform.

CRISP-DM is a how-to guide. It describes the steps needed to gain valuable insight into your data. While it does not go into the details of areas like machine learning, it does identify the steps necessary to gather, clean, and organize data for proper analysis. As a result, many machine learning tutorials, techniques, and other books follow the guidelines outlined in the CRISP-DM guide whether they intended to do so or not.

If you and your organization are just starting out to create an enrichment platform such that it can be used by knowledge workers reviewing these documents will prepare you mentally for the challenges that you will be facing. Becoming familiar with these guides will be the giants whose shoulders you stand on when creating your enrichment platform.

Bibliography

Blokdyk, Gerardus. 2018. *Gerardus Blokdyk*. 5STARCooks.

Collins, Jim. 2001. *Good to Great*. New York: HarperBusiness.

DAMA International. 2017. *Data Management Body of Knowledge*. 2nd ed. Basking Ridge, NJ: Technics Publications.

n.d. *https://medium.com/the-innovation/the-missing-bullet-holes-and-abraham-wald-25e68d7a870f*.

n.d. *https://www.kimballgroup.com/2010/10/design-tip-128-selecting-default-values-for-nulls/*.

Inmon, W. H. 1999. *Building the Operational Data Store*. Danvers, MA: John Wiley & Sons, Inc.

Laney, Douglas B. 2018. *Infonomics: How to Monetize, Manage, and Measure Information as an Asset for Competitive Advantage*. New York: Bibliomotion, Inc.

Needham, Doug. n.d. "Data Structure Graph: The Application of Graph Theory to the Design and Implementation of a Relational Data Model." *Academia.org*. Accessed June 4, 2021. https://www.academia.edu/42186606/Data_Structure_Grap

h_The_Application_of_Graph_Theory_to_the_Design_and _Implementation_of_a_Relational_Data_Model.

—. 2015. *Data Structure Graphs: The Structure of Your Data Has Meaning.*

Oxford. n.d. *Enrichment.* Accessed June 3, 2021. https://www.lexico.com/en/definition/enrichment.

Vigen, Tyler. n.d. *Spurious Correlations.* Accessed June 13, 2021. https://tylervigen.com/view_correlation?id=598.

Index

www.ingramcontent.com/pod-product-compliance
Lightning Source LLC
Chambersburg PA
CBHW071245050326
40690CB00011B/2273